KIRK BY DIVINE RIGHT

KIRK BY DIVINE RIGHT

Church and State: peaceful co-existence

The Baird Lectures 1985

Andrew Herron

THE SAINT ANDREW PRESS: EDINBURGH

First published in 1985 by
THE SAINT ANDREW PRESS
121 George Street, Edinburgh EH2 4YN

Copyright © Andrew Herron 1985

All rights reserved. No part of this publication may be reproduced or transmitted in any form or by any means, electronic or mechanical, including photocopy, recording, or information storage and retrieval system, without permission in writing from the publisher. This book is sold subject to the condition that it shall not, by way of trade or otherwise, be lent, resold, hired out or otherwise circulated without the publisher's prior consent.

British Library Cataloguing in Publication data
Herron, Andrew
 Kirk by divine right: church and state:
 peaceful coexistence.
 1. Church of Scotland — History 2. Church and
 state — Scotland — History 3. Scotland —
 Church history
 I. Title
 322'.1'0941   BX9070

ISBN 0-7152-0588-9

Printed in Great Britain by Bell and Bain Ltd., Glasgow

Contents

Page

Chapter I	Introduction: The Crown Rights of Christ	7
Chapter II	The Kirk, the Crown, the Covenant and the Conventicle	22
Chapter III	Kirk Creed and Christian Conscience	47
Chapter IV	Auld Lichts an' a' That	68
Chapter V	Courts of the Kirk and Courts of the Kingdom	89
Chapter VI	The Contemporary Kirk	109
Index		129

I

Introduction: The Crown Rights of Christ

Sole Judge
To anyone at all intimately associated with the life of the Church of Scotland these words must strike a familiar note, for they are heard at every service of admission to office within the Kirk. They appear as the predicate in the clause '... of which agreement the Church itself shall be sole judge'; and that in turn comes as the culmination of a claim on behalf of the Church that it has the right to formulate, interpret, or modify its standards, subject to the restriction only that such alteration shall be in agreement with the Word of God and the fundamental doctrines of the faith — 'of which agreement the Church itself shall be sole judge'.

The words have a grandly sonorous ring to them, but, far more important, they resound with a finality that brooks neither doubt nor denial — objections are swept aside, the subject is closed, there is no more to be said — unless, perhaps, it be a Threefold Amen!

It must be immediately apparent that this is a stupendous claim the Kirk is making — a claim not only to be mistress in her own household, but to be judge in her own cause. These represent two entirely different positions. The claim to be master in your own household would be generally conceded to be right and reasonable; the claim to be judge in your own cause would be universally regarded as unreasonable and unjust. It is my contention, however, that the Kirk is going even farther than that: the Kirk is not just claiming to be sole judge of issues which fall within her proper sphere, she is demanding also to be sole judge in determining what are the limits of that proper sphere. Throughout the four centuries of the history of the Church of Scotland this attitude has been one of its most important and significant characteristics. Taken along with the Scotsman's passion for law — indeed genius as a lawyer — it has done much to shape the pattern and to determine the history of the Kirk.

It is my hope in these pages to develop this theme and to show how the claim to be sole judge has brought the Kirk into conflict, first of all with the Crown, then with the conscience of the individual, then with the courts of the realm, and now with some of today's popular movements in the Church. First, though, I must set the doctrine of 'sole judge' in its constitutional context.

The Preamble

As noted above, the words are well known because of their appearance in the preamble[1] that is read in face of the congregation on all occasions of admission to office within the Kirk. Having reaffirmed the Kirk's adherence to the Gospel of the redeeming love of Christ, and having acknowledged the Scriptures of the Old and New Testaments to be the supreme rule of life, the preamble goes on to an acceptance of the Westminster Confession as the Kirk's subordinate standard, 'recognising liberty of opinion on such points of doctrine as do not enter into the substance of the Faith, and claiming the right, in dependence on the promised guidance of the Holy Spirit, to formulate, interpret, or modify its subordinate standards: always in agreement with the Word of God and the fundamental doctrines of the Christian faith contained in the said Confession — of which agreement the Church itself shall be sole judge'.

Oddly enough, none of the questions put to the candidate following upon the reading of the preamble reflects this claim of the Kirk to be sole judge — he is not required to accept that position or to submit himself to that kind of judicature. The nearest he comes to that is an undertaking to make himself subject to the Presbytery and to the superior courts of the Church. But it seems clear that you could be abjectly obedient to the General Assembly while at the same time claiming that in certain matters there was a court of higher jurisdiction to which you could refer your cause — here and not just hereafter!

The Articles Declaratory

The preamble, of course, is in its turn an echo of the

INTRODUCTION

appropriate section of the Articles Declaratory, and it is necessary that we should look with some care at these. Their full title is 'Articles Declaratory of the Constitution of the Church of Scotland in Matters Spiritual',[2] and they are incorporated in an Act of Parliament, the Church of Scotland Act 1921. The Articles had been prepared in anticipation of the union of the Church of Scotland with the United Free Church of Scotland which took place in 1929 — and they are represented as being wholly declaratory in character — that is to say, they do not create a new situation, they merely tell us clearly what the existing situation is. It should perhaps be remarked in passing that this may not in fact be completely true, as the majority decision in the Kirkmabreck case of 1936[3] established — but more of that hereafter. In 1919 the Articles had been approved by a very large majority of Presbyteries; they were subsequently approved by both Houses of Parliament; and they received the Royal Assent on 28 July 1921. Their becoming effective was delayed till they had again obtained Presbytery approval and until another Bill relating to property and endowments had become an Act, so that it was not until 28 June 1926 that an Order in Council made the Articles operative.

Apart from setting forth a summary of the Kirk's doctrinal position, the Articles represent a repeated declaration of its absolute autonomy. Let us look at some of them in detail.

Article IV affirms 'the right and power of the Kirk, subject to no civil authority, to adjudicate finally in all matters of doctrine, worship, government and discipline in the Church, including questions of membership and office, constitution and membership of courts, mode of election of office-bearers and determining the boundaries of the sphere of labour of its ministers and other office-bearers.' Note that the power is 'to adjudicate finally'. The Article then goes on specifically and emphatically to make the point that the recognition of such rights by the civil authority does not mean that they are, or ever have been, conferred by such authority — they derive from the Divine King and Head of the Church and from Him alone. What these Articles are purporting to do is to define the Kirk's position 'in matters spiritual'. Yet it must be manifest that the ramifications of most of the issues specified in this particular Article extend far beyond the purely spiritual dimension. But the claim to be sole judge is still there, even if in this instance it is described as the right 'to adjudicate finally'.

Article V in equally unyielding terms claims 'the inherent right free from interference from civil authority' to frame and adopt, modify or formulate new doctrinal statements, accepting, naturally, that all such alterations must be agreeable to the Word of God and the fundamental doctrines of the Christian faith contained in the Confession, but insisting that in all questions regarding such agreement the Church itself is to be sole judge. It is most interesting that the Article goes on to allow 'due regard to liberty of opinion in points which do not enter into the substance of the Faith' — but the context makes it abundantly clear that in determining what are those 'points that do not enter into the substance of the Faith' the Church itself is to be sole judge — as also, no doubt, in the decision of what constitutes the 'due regard' that is to be paid to liberty of opinion.

Article VII recognises that there is an obligation upon the Church to seek and promote union with denominations where the Word is purely preached, the Sacraments truly administered, and discipline rightly exercised, and that it is free to unite with such a Church without loss of identity 'on terms which this Church finds to be consistent with these Articles'. What that amounts to in simple terms is that before any such incorporating union can be achieved two formidable hurdles have to be cleared — first the Kirk has to be satisfied that in the other denomination preaching, sacraments, and discipline are sound, and secondly that the terms of the union are consistent with the Articles. And in respect of the answers to these two questions it is the Kirk and the Kirk alone that will decide.

It must be evident, then, that the Articles Declaratory represent to a quite peculiar degree an affirmation by the Kirk of her absolute authority within her own domain. What precisely are the bounds of that domain is not made clear — what is made crystal clear is that in any question on this subject the Church itself is to be sole judge. So that in effect the Kirk is to be autonomous within her own borders and a law unto herself within the State.

It is interesting that in 1906 the United Free Church (just

six years old at the time) passed an Act anent the Spiritual Independence of the Church in which it was declared and enacted that the Church had the sole and exclusive right and power from time to time to alter, change, add to, or modify her constitution and laws, subordinate standards and formulas, and to determine and declare what these are, always in conformity with the Word of God and the basic rules of the Church itself — 'of which conformity the Church herself, acting through her courts, shall be sole judge'. Whatever lingering differences may in 1929 still have separated the two branches of the Kirk they could not conceivably have been more at one in respect of the claim that the Kirk was to be not merely mistress in her own household, but sole judge in her own household, and sole judge too of what were the matters pertaining to her own household. A stupendous claim, indeed.

Church and State

Before leaving the subject of the Articles Declaratory it is important to draw attention to Article VI which specifically deals, however briefly, with the relationship of Church and State. The Article begins by acknowledging the divine appointment and authority of the civil magistrate within his own sphere, and it goes on to say that 'the Church and State owe mutual duties to each other, and acting within their respective spheres may signally promote each other's welfare'. Then it makes the somewhat astonishing statement, 'The Church and State have the right to determine each for itself all questions concerning the extent and the continuance of their mutual relations in the discharge of their duties and the obligations arising therefrom'.

Whatever may be thought of this as a contribution towards solving the thorny problem of Church–State relations, no-one could possibly see it as representing any serious concession by the Kirk of its claim to autonomy *vis-à-vis* the State. The suggestion that two parties who may well be in bitter conflict on some subject are entitled each for itself to determine what are the rights and wrongs of that subject rather takes one's breath away. It was this kind of attitude which created the deadlock; it was, in fact, bound to do so. The existence of one sole judge raises problems enough to be disturbing; the thought of two sole judges operating simultaneously in the same field is positively terrifying.

That apart, the Article seems to suggest that all will be well between Church and State if each accepts the doctrine of 'rendering unto Caesar the things that are Caesar's and unto God the things that are God's.' This, I submit, is a remarkably unhelpful principle. You remember the occasion that elicited the dictum. Some smart alecs had set out to impale our Lord on the horns of a dilemma. 'Tell us,' they enquired with an air of disarming innocence, 'is it lawful to pay tribute to Caesar?' An obvious pitfall. Let Jesus say 'Yes' and He is in trouble with the Jewish leaders who refuse to recognise Roman rule as lawful: let Him say 'No' and He will instantly be reported to the Roman authorities as a trouble-maker inciting the people to withhold their taxes. As we all know, our Lord was equal to the occasion. Cleverly He turned the horns of the dilemma by pointing out that Caesar's head appeared on the coinage and that men should render unto Caesar the things that are Caesar's and unto God the things that are God's. His tormentors were confounded — beaten on their home-ground. It is essential, though, to keep in mind that these were the circumstances in which the dictum was pronounced. Our Lord was not propounding a system of Church–State relationship. He merely turned the horns of a dilemma — He did not dehorn it. The dilemma is still with us; the questions have still to be answered, What are the things that are Caesar's? What are the things that are God's? And as soon as an answer has been found for these a further supremely important question emerges — in any matter of dispute as to where the line of demarcation is to be drawn who is to be judge, Caesar or God? And what of the situation where both Caesar and God seem to have valid claims upon our allegiance but are directing us in different ways — to whom is absolute obedience due?

In this intensely confused and difficult sphere the Kirk has all along been guided by an unswerving allegiance to the doctrine of the Crown Rights of Christ and accordingly has never known what it was so much as to doubt the validity of her claim to absolute autonomy.

'All Due Assistance'

The conviction that she is completely free of any kind or degree of State control has naturally been strengthened by a provision in the Revolution Settlement Act of 1693 to the effect that 'magistrates, judges, and officers of judgment shall give all due assistance for making the sentences and censures of the Church and judicatories thereof to be obeyed'. Not only are the Church courts to be free from interference from the civil arm, they are entitled to call for the intervention of the civil arm in their support. It was in 1874 that a case arose in the Presbytery of Lewis where a witness who had been cited to testify in a libel failed to appear, and the Sheriff declined to pass an order to compel his attendance. The matter was appealed to the Court of Session where the requisite order was given by Lord President Inglis who prefaced his judgment with the remark, 'I was surprised to see this question raised, for I never during the whole course of my practice entertained a doubt' on it. He quoted the passage from the Act of 1693 referred to above, and then went on, 'I want nothing stronger or more comprehensive that that. Whenever the Church courts are unable of themselves to carry out their own orders made to explicate their own jurisdiction, the civil courts are bound to step in and give "all due assistance"'.[4] Oddly enough, this seems to be the last recorded case of such assistance being sought.

I can, however, contribute a quite illuminating incident from my own experience. Very shortly after I had become Clerk to the Presbytery of Glasgow we found ourselves engaged in a libel affecting the conduct of a minister, and, as the law requires, we dealt with the case behind closed doors. Later we issued a short statement to the press. Next day one newspaper carried a full, detailed report of our private meeting. I wrote to the editor suggesting, quite politely, that this appeared to me a serious breach of the etiquette I had come to expect from the press, and seeking an assurance that it would not be repeated. I received a reply in terms not at all polite, telling me quite simply to 'get lost'. In answering I referred to the Act and to the Lewis case and indicated that failing receipt of the assurance sought we proposed to raise an action of interdict to prevent his newspaper reporting further on the case. This obviously went to his legal advisers and produced from the editor a most abject apology and a firm promise that the offence would not be repeated. For the information — and edification — of the press bench generally I reported rather fully on the matter at the next meeting of the Presbytery, and The Glasgow Herald followed up with a leader-page spread 'From our Court of Session Correspondent' who upheld our position to the full and going on to point out some of the dire consequences that could have followed upon the editor continuing on his evil courses. So the Act seems still to be very much alive.

There were those who would have invoked it in 1970 when for the first time the General Assembly invited the attendance of a Roman Catholic 'visitor'. There was the threat of a demonstration in the Public Gallery, and this in fact occurred. I recollect the suggestion being advanced that this ought not to be treated as a simple breach of the peace but on the same basis as if it had occurred down the street at the Sheriff Court. This would almost certainly have been an ill-advised course to follow. In 1693 when the Act was passed it would have been quite unthinkable that the courts of the Church would become involved in all the multifarious administrative and other functions that now engage their attention, and in my view it would be unreasonable to expect the kind of aid envisaged from the civil arm in any other than their patently judicatory functions.

Before we pass from this subject, though, it is of interest to note that in the Presbytery of Lewis affair Lord President Inglis also made the following observation *à propos* the peculiar position of the courts of the Kirk:

> We are dealing with a Presbytery, an established judicature of the country, as much recognised by law as the Court of Session itself. Its jurisdiction, indeed, differs widely from that of the civil courts, but it is just as much the creation of law as that of any other court of the kingdom.

This followed upon and confirmed an equally emphatic statement made four years earlier in 1870 by Lord Justice Clerk Moncrieff in a case where the Presbytery of Dunkeld had been ordered by the General Assembly to deal with certain charges against the minister of Auchtergaven which had not been pursued at the time when the original libel was

INTRODUCTION

tried, and where the minister, pleading that he had tholed his assize, sought the intervention of the civil court in his defence. His Lordship said:

> If, therefore, this were a case in which we were called upon to review the proceedings of an inferior court, I should have thought that a strong case had been made out for our interference. But whatever inconsiderate dicta may have been thrown out to that effect, that is not the law of Scotland. The jurisdiction of the Church Courts, as recognised judicatories of this realm, rests on a similar statutory foundation to that under which we administer justice within these walls. It is easy to suggest extravagant instances of excess of power, but quite as easy to do so in regard to the one jurisdiction as to the other. Within their province the Church Courts are as supreme as we are within the civil; and as this is a matter relating to the discipline of the Church, and solely within the discipline of the Church Courts, I think that we have no power whatever to interfere.[5]

In 1985 there was raised in the Court of Session an action of interdict which involved this whole question of jurisdiction. The facts briefly were these — a Presbytery had taken action against one of its ministers in terms of the Act anent Congregations in an Unsatisfactory State and finding that he was substantially responsible for the said state had dissolved the pastoral tie; the minister had appealed to the Judicial Commission of Assembly which had heard and dismissed the appeal without, as was later discovered, having a full quorum present; the General Assembly had then sent the matter back to the Judicial Commission for report to next Assembly. The Court of Session was asked to grant interdict to prevent this happening. As it transpired the issue of jurisdiction was not fully presented from the side of the petitioner so that the Lord Ordinary was able to dismiss the case in a single sentence. From our point of view this was an unfortunate outcome, for the case did provide an excellent forum for this important age-old issue to be debated in the light of modern thinking; but what really matters is that the Kirk's position stands unshaken.

In view of all this it is not surprising that in face of all opposition, generally at great cost to herself, and frequently torn by dissension from within as well as battered by persecution from without, she had stood fast by her claim to be sole judge. It is a claim which over the years has cost the Kirk dear, a claim which has involved her in many a conflict, but a claim which even in her darkest hour she has never dreamt of conceding, and a claim to which she still adheres today, and that as firmly as ever.

Kirk against King

It is these conflicts into which her claim to autonomy has brought her over the years that form the topic of this volume. So I shall at this stage indicate briefly the line that I propose to follow.

First of all the Kirk's insistence on her autonomy brought her into bitter and long-drawn conflict with the Crown. For at least a century war was waged on a series of battlefronts between the Kirk and the Stuart kings. It could not be said of the Crown Rights of Christ and the Divine Right of Kings that never the twain did meet — it could be said that every time they met sparks were sure to fly. There need be no difficulty in understanding the passionate affection of the Stuart kings for the doctrine of Divine Right — after all it was the only foundation capable of supporting the kind of absolute monarchy they were determined to exercise in an age characterised by a swelling tide of democratic aspiration. The one reason why the king was on the throne was that in the inscrutable wisdom of God it had been ordained that he should know better than Parliament or General Assembly or any other collection of his subjects what was good for his people, what indeed was God's will for the nation. You could not ask for anything simpler than that. After 1603 south of the border the Stuarts fought with a Parliament which claimed to speak with the voice of the people; north of the border their quarrel was with a Kirk which had a democratic constitution of sorts, but whose claim was that it spoke with the voice of God. There just had to be trouble.

And of course there was. Plenty of it. A struggle that began almost immediately after the Reformation in the days of the regency of Mary of Guise, that girned on like the proverbial sore tooth throughout the reign of King James VI and I, that gathered strength and gained fresh urgency with the aspirations of Charles I, that came to a head with the Covenants, that ebbed and flowed as 'killing times' were interrupted by 'blinks', with spells of persecution and periods of toleration, that saw a king beheaded and that found Cromwell a fickle friend, and that was not brought to an end till 1690 when Presbyterianism finally triumphed and since when every sovereign on his accession is required to swear an oath that he will maintain the Protestant faith and Presbyterian Church government within the realm of Scotland.

The round, it could be said, had indisputably been won by the Kirk. But at what a cost, and what a heritage it left — for instance, what we should nowadays refer to as the side-effects of the Covenants were to plague the Kirk for many a generation to come. This struggle forms the subject of Chapter 2.

Kirk Against Conscience

With the second area of conflict, I deal in Chapter 3, and that centres around the contest witnessed in the mid-18th century between the dictate of the Kirk and the conscience of the individual — how far did authority run when it ran contrary to deep personal conviction. Having substantially won the battle against absolute monarchy, the Kirk found herself confronted with some of the results of her own victory in what might be called absolute democracy. As representative of a general position two particular cases stand out sharply, those of Ebenezer Erskine and Thomas Gillespie, founders respectively of the Associate Synod and the Presbytery of Relief, the two bodies which in 1847, after many strange adventures by the way, were to come together to form the United Presbyterian Church — 'the UPs'. On a cursory reading of the history of the cases one could be forgiven for attributing both of these considerable secessions from the Establishment to the harmful effects of the Law of Patronage — and there are those who have done so. Was it not over a proposed Act giving rights to heritors in the selection of ministers in the one instance, and over a disputed settlement in the other, that the issue was joined between the Kirk and the individual protester? But however many pressures may have been involved — trends in theology, differing views on the relation between Church and State, a hatred of the operation of the Law of Patronage — the nub of the matter was a confrontation between the Kirk taking up an official stand and the conscience of the individual Christian believer dictating otherwise. Erskine claimed that he was entitled, if conscience so demanded, to preach, at the opening of a Synod which had appointed him its Moderator, a sermon bitterly critical of the General Assembly. Gillespie, on the other hand, claimed that though the General Assembly might enjoin him as a member of Presbytery to be present at a service of induction the voice of conscience that forbade him to have part or lot in such a service was the voice to which he must pay heed. Here, then, the battle raged — Kirk versus conscience.

Fragmentation

My contention in Chapter 4 will be that those who went out with the Erskines in the Secession over the issue of conscience ultimately defeated their own purpose because their doctrine being carried to its full logical conclusion started a process of fragmentation which on their own principles they were unable to halt — a movement that threatened the very existence of the Secession Church. Increasingly it became clear that if each man's conscience was to be the measure of truth, and if the Church must enshrine the whole truth as so conceived, then the day must ultimately come when there were as many denominations as there were individual Christians. We shall see too how congregations no less than the Church itself became infected with this passion for separation. Mercifully the fragmenting ceased and a period of reunion ensued. The Kirk might be said to have won that round through exhaustion and dissension in the ranks of the enemy, even if it was at the expense of the introduction of the clause allowing 'liberty of opinion on such points of doctrine as do not enter into the substance of the Faith'. Considering that the Kirk herself was to be sole judge of what these points of doctrine were, this was a concession of no great significance.

Before Their Lordships

The third major area of conflict — covered in Chapter 5 — I describe as the Courts of the Kirk and the Courts of the

Kingdom. This particular confrontation took place in the courts of the land, principally in the Court of Session and the House of Lords and was almost wholly concentrated within the period 1833–43. When this is referred to, as it often is, as 'The Ten Years' Conflict' the struggle generally envisaged is that between the Moderate and the Evangelical or Non-Intrusion elements within the Church itself throughout that crucial period. The title, however, is an admirable one to describe the tension between the Church and the courts on what in the last resort was the Kirk's claim to autonomy — to be sole judge. The actual cases, of course, had to do with the operation of patronage — with the old question whether a congregation had to accept the presentee of the patron or whether they themselves had a right of choice — or at the very least a right of veto. But, as was to be expected, the issues went much deeper than that. There was, for example, the question whether the courts should have any jurisdiction at all in a matter so obviously a spiritual matter as the choice of a minister to fill a vacancy. Again there was the interesting if rather half-hearted attempt to find a solution by drawing a neat line between the spiritual and the temporal elements in the ministry of a parish. Or again there was the question as to the extent of the freedom of the Church in matters where the State claimed a concurrent jurisdiction — the Chapel Act was a particularly glaring example of legislation by the Assembly which ignored the provisions of statute law on the same subject.

This round, it must be freely admitted, went against the Kirk. As we all know, a very large minority, not being prepared to accept such a conclusion, walked out of the Establishment in 1843 and founded the Free Church of Scotland. However, the outcome of the Cardross cases of 1859, and even more emphatically the result of the Free Church case of 1904, proved how illusory had been the freedom from intervention by the courts of the kingdom achieved in consequence of the Disruption; it proved that the only difference distinguishing the Auld Kirk from the Free Kirk in this regard was that in the former case a dent had been made in the Kirk's armour against Their Lordships while in the latter case the Kirk stood defenceless in the dock.

The Contemporary Scene
The final chapter I devote to an attempt to bring things up to date and even, perhaps, greatly daring, to venture a glimpse into the future, my object throughout being, naturally, the limited one of seeing how the Kirk's claim to autonomy can be fitted into the changing scene and attempting to see how far the idea of a Kirk by Divine Right is a relevant concept in today's world.

There is, it appears to me, a tendency towards congregationalism developing within the Kirk — an understandable enough reaction by congregations against the ever-increasing pressures, particularly but not exclusively of a financial kind, that are being imposed from above. Initiative at the parish level is relentlessly being eroded. This is resented, and we still have our secessions. Also at the congregational level, the question has to be asked whether the Kirk is sufficiently democratic to satisfy contemporary demands in this direction. Often one hears the boast that ours is a democratic Church. I have always maintained that this is not true. Our system of government is Presbyterian, not democratic, and they are not the same thing, very far from it. In the 16th century when Presbyterianism was established it must, to the people of that day, have appeared as a miracle of democracy, partly in its freedom from priestly domination and partly in the place given in its councils to the common man. The trouble is that it has changed very little in these four centuries whereas the popular conception of democracy has altered out of all recognition. Where does all this leave us today?

Moreover the charge is frequently heard these days that the Kirk is less and less governed on a conciliar basis and is fast becoming a bureaucracy. Courts are giving place to Committees. Our headquarters are no longer in Heaven — they have moved to 121 George Street. For us the question must have considerable importance for it involves the issue of what exactly is this Church that is to be sole judge.

One of the most fascinating phenomena on the contemporary ecclesiastical scene is 'the ecumenical body' — the World Council of Churches, the British Council of Churches, the World Alliance of Reformed Churches, and so on. With the passing of the years these bodies, modest enough in their original conception, are taking increasing initiatives as autonomous bodies, are speaking in name of 'the Churches' if not actually of 'the Church'. This, of course, raises a vitally important question as to how far they are entitled so to do. How deeply are the constituent denominations committed by the activities and pronouncements of these Councils, how far have they sacrificed their sovereignty in belonging to these Councils? There is here a wide field for study — and in my view an urgent need for such study to be undertaken.

Finally, something must be said, however cursorily, about the ecumenical movement itself and its implications for a Kirk which claims to be the Kirk of a nation and to be sole judge in all its affairs.

References
1 Cox, JT (1934). *Practice and Procedure in the Church of Scotland.* The Committee on General Administration, Church of Scotland, Sixth edn (1976), p571.
2 *Ibid*, p471.
3 Ballantyne v Presbytery of Wigtown — 1936 SC, p625.
4 Presbytery of Lewis v Fraser (1875), 1R888.
5 Wight v Presbytery of Dunkeld (1870), 8M, p925.

II

The Kirk, the Crown, the Covenant and the Conventicle

The Accession Oath

'A deputation entered the throne-room to tell the Queen that everything was ready.' So says an account of how, just two days after the death of King George VI the new monarch took the oath to maintain Presbyterian Church Government in Scotland. 'Thereafter,' the account goes on, 'Her Majesty entered alone to meet the assembled counsellors. The first thing she did was to read her Accession Declaration; then she assented to the request of the Lord President that it should be published. Immediately the Lord President handed Her Majesty a copy of the Oath relating to the security of the Church of Scotland together with a copy of the New Testament bound in black leather. The Queen proceeded to take the oath:

> I Elizabeth the Second by the grace of God of Great Britain, Ireland, and the British Dominions beyond the Seas, Queen, Defender of the Faith, do faithfully promise and swear that I shall inviolably maintain and preserve the Settlement of the true Protestant Religion as established by the Laws made in Scotland in prosecution of the Claim of Right, and particularly by an Act intituled an Act for securing the Protestant Religion and Presbyterian Church Government and by the Acts passed in the Parliament of both Kingdoms for union of the two kingdoms, together with the Worship, Discipline, Rights and Privileges of the Church of Scotland. So help me God.

With the words, "This I gladly do" spoken of her own accord, the Queen then took the oath and appended her signature.'[1]

This simple ceremony, performed now by 13 successive monarchs, highlights the outcome of a long period of the most bitter struggle between Kirk and Crown, a fight that raged for more than a century, beginning soon after the Reformation of 1560 and continuing until the Revolution Settlement of 1690, a contest that embraced various attempts to introduce bishops and to impose a prayer book, a struggle that produced the Covenants and the Covenanters, that saw the outing of ministers and the rabbling of curates, that gathered the conventicles, that saw men praying ahint dykes and that saw men shot ahint dykes, that watched an old body and a young lassie drown in Solway tide — and all over the question of what was meant by the Crown Rights of Christ.

In the end it was the Kirk that won the day, and each new monarch solemnly swears that not by him shall the battle be again engaged.

If the Accession Oath is thus the constitutional guarantee of the fruits of the Kirk's ultimate victory in that costly contest, the popular and obvious symbol of it lies in the presence at each Assembly of His Grace the Lord High Commissioner. In the court but not of it, speaking only when spoken to, accorded all the deference due to sovereignty itself but powerless to intervene in the Assembly's affairs, and at the close invited to inform Her Majesty that the Assembly have appointed their next meeting to be holden at Edinburgh on a certain date — this is the position today of a King's man whose teeth have all been drawn. In claiming and being granted the right to appoint a commissioner Jamie the Saxt had been quick to see the possibility of directing the business of the Kirk, but the Assembly saw to it that the commissioner's brief should be a watching brief, that the King's Commissioner should be but a spectator.

This chapter tries to trace, however sketchily, the steps by which this present position — thought by many to represent the best balance ever reached between Church and State — came to be established, and begins with the events leading to the appearance in 1564 of the First Book of Discipline.

The Scottish Reformation

As we all know, the Reformation in Europe can be said to have begun on 31 October 1517, the day that Martin Luther nailed his 95 theses to the door of the Church in Wittenberg. It was against the abuses, represented by the sale of indulgences, that Luther directed his theses, but it was, of course, the positive contribution he made to religious thought, particularly in his message about justification by faith and in his doctrine of the priesthood of all believers, that he gave to the Reformation its direction and to the new Church its inspiration and ultimately its theology.

It was to be some time before the impact of the movement reached our Scottish shores, but this it did in quite dramatic fashion with the burning of Patrick Hamilton. It was as a student in Paris, Louvain and Marburg that Patrick Hamilton, the brilliant son of a distinguished family, came under the influence of the new thought, and he fell a complete victim to its power so that on his return to his native land in 1527 he immediately set about the proclamation of the Gospel, the new free Gospel. Word of what he was doing spread, and very soon he was invited by the authorities to come to St Andrews where he might expound his views, and this he did to such effect that he was arrested, tried, condemned as a heretic and burned at the stake in February 1528, at the age of 25. As might have been expected, the main effect of this brutal act was to direct attention to Hamilton's teaching — so much so it came to be said that if others were to be treated in like fashion the burning should be done in cellars, 'for the reek of Patrick Hamilton had infected all it blew upon'.

After this, Reformation teaching relentlessly spread. Tyndale's New Testament, smuggled across from Holland, was in many hands. Parliament in 1543 went so far as to make lawful the reading of the Bible in the vulgar tongue. On the negative side the inadequacies and abuses of the Roman Church were receiving the most damning publicity in popular literature. It was upon this scene that George Wishart entered when, on his return from Switzerland and Germany, he began to preach in Dundee, the Lothians and elsewhere. Among the first to be attracted to his cause was one John Knox. Unhappily Wishart's ministry was to be of short duration for he was arrested, taken to St Andrews, and on 1 March 1546 he suffered the fate that had overtaken Patrick Hamilton 18 years earlier. It is said that on the night of his arrest he had sent Knox away with the awful premonition, 'One is sufficient for a sacrifice.'

The moving spirit behind the arrest and death of Wishart had been Cardinal David Beaton, a man of great experience and undoubted ability but void of integrity, an outstanding ecclesiastic with little concern for the things of the faith, a man deeply committed to salvage the falling Church but unconcerned about its errors and corruptions. Soon after the death of Wishart a plot was hatched against Beaton and he was cruelly murdered in his castle of St Andrews. 'Although the loon was well away, the deed was foully done.'

John Knox

It was at this point that John Knox came to the forefront of Scotland's Reformation. He joined those gathered for safety in the Castle of St Andrews following on Beaton's death, and it was from here that he was carried off to serve for 18 months at the oars of a French man-o'-war. Peace with France led to his release and he returned to England to be minister in the town of Berwick. The year 1553 saw Mary Tudor ascend the throne of England, and it was in company with thousands of others that Knox fled the country. It was thus he was brought into contact with that great reformer, John Calvin, under whose influence he fell, gaining deep insights into the doctrine, worship and government which Calvin had devised for the Church organised by him at Geneva. It was here too that we find the root of the doctrine of the autonomy of the Kirk which Knox was to imprint on the Scottish Church and which would characterise it throughout its history. For Calvin had based his doctrine of the Church upon what through his study of Scripture he had been led to believe was the mind of Christ — to wit, the sovereignty of God, with its attendant theory of the Crown Rights of Christ. The worship of the Church was stripped of ceremony, its government found a place for the layman, the rule of bishops was rejected as bringing the Church under State control and creating clerical tyranny. Heavily impregnated with these ideas, John Knox returned to his own land to become the key figure in the Reformation there.

The Auld Alliance with France was coming under severe strain at this time. Mary of Guise, regent for her young daughter Mary, was completely French in outlook and it was becoming evident that Scotland would soon be little better than a province of France. This did not appeal to the *amour propre* of the Scot, and, besides, there was now this deep religious division. So the party of the Reformation looked with increasing favour towards England where Elizabeth now ruled, and in 1559, soon after the death of the Regent, Elizabeth sent an army north, obliging the French to depart and leaving the leaders of the Reformation to take control.

All now seemed set fair for reform. The control of Scottish affairs lay with the Lords of the Congregation, the Protestant leaders who were committed 'to maintain, set forward and establish the most blessed Word of God and His congregation'. It is sadly true that many of these noble gentlemen were more interested in extending the bounds of their own estates at the expense of Kirk lands than they were in the dissemination of the Gospel; it is no less sadly true that among the commonality of the people there was an element which, having suffered under the oppression of the old regime and having had ample opportunity to form exaggerated impressions of the evil and godless character of many of its leaders, were more anxious to 'have a bash' by breaking and burning and rioting than they were to see a brave new Church erected out of what could be salvaged from the old. But too much can be, and has been, made of these aspects. The Scottish Reformation sprang from the ground and for that reason was deeply rooted; it was inspired by the desire of ordinary folk to have a Church in which they could put their trust, and for that reason there was demanded the closest scrutiny and the most ruthless purging of all that had been before. In this the Scottish Reformation differed completely from its English counterpart where the king set himself up in place of the pope, spoiled the religious houses, but otherwise encouraged the continuance of business as usual. And then too at the head of the movement in Scotland there was John Knox, preaching consistently of the new opportunities, presenting the fresh challenge, and, above all, declaring the Kingship of Christ. More and more the Reformation took hold upon the decent folk of Scotland, putting the Bible into their hands, teaching them to sing the Psalms, setting before them high moral standards, and giving them faith in themselves as the children of God, as the new priesthood, as the heirs to the promises.

Scotland Reformed

By 1559 the Reformation may be said to have been achieved in fact if not on paper and it was therefore appropriate that legislation should go on the statute-book — of both Church and State. The use of the Latin mass was officially abolished by Parliament, as was the entire Episcopal system of government. A Confession of Faith was adopted, the famous *Scots Confession of 1560* which, incidentally, has recently gained a new prominence in consequence of the suggestion by the Panel on Doctrine that it should be formally adopted by the Church as one of its 'chief subordinate standards'.[2] As is well known, this Confession was the work of six 'Johns', was compiled within a few days, owed a good deal to Calvin's Institutes, and was securely founded upon God's Holy Word as the authors so emphatically declared. This also received the formal approval of Parliament.

The Confession was followed by *The First Book of Discipline*, the work of the same six 'Johns', being the draft for a pattern of Church government. Necessarily this was an incomplete document which could not at this stage be put to any practical test. There was still no adequate supply of ministers; thanks to the depredations of the nobility there was a complete shortage of funds; and, obviously, there was no first-hand experience to found upon. The book, however, set forth some principles very clearly, among them the doctrine that the ministry of the Church belongs equally to 'the labourers and manurers of the earth as to the nobles' — a doctrine that was to stand as a bulwark against the attempt to introduce Episcopacy in days to come. Then the year 1564 saw the adoption of Knox's Book of Common Order. So, from a legal point of view, in matters of doctrine, worship and government the Church was now equipped with writing which enjoyed the imprimatur of Parliament.

It is of no little interest that all these standards were confirmed by Parliament. To that extent, apparently, the Kirk was prepared to concede the right of the State to meddle in her affairs. What might have happened had Parliament declined to approve or had insisted on introducing amendments it is interesting to conjecture. Such a situation is, however, largely a hypothetical one, for at that time when membership of the nation and of the Church were practically coterminous such a disagreement could not have arisen. History had not yet reached the position where the House of Commons could throw out a proposed new Prayer Book for the Church of England. And, thanks to the tenacity with which our fathers held to their position as sole judge, such a situation has never arisen for us, and it is difficult to see how it could.

According to the Scots Confession the marks of a true Church are the true preaching of the Word, the right administration of the Sacraments, and the upright exercising of discipline. But who was to say how far any or all of these things were being achieved? To any of the six 'Johns' it would have been quite unthinkable that the king should presume to act as arbiter or that any court of the realm should sit as judge on such an issue. It was the Kirk herself who should say, the Kirk herself who would be sole judge. They did not say so. To them it was obvious, and the obvious does not need to be written into a statute — or at least not in those days!

Here already at the very founding of the Scottish Kirk we meet the principle that will confront us at every turn, that the Kirk is there by Divine Right, that she owes allegiance first and foremost to her only King and Head, Jesus Christ, and that in all matters that concern her she shall herself be sole judge.

Andrew Melville

After the brief, unhappy reign of Mary, and the assassination of Moray in 1570, Morton became regent for the young James VI. Morton, it would seem, held the intriguing view that the General Assembly was a body designed to exercise that ecclesiastic supremacy which would in normal circumstances have been exercised by the Queen — had she not been a Catholic. From this it followed that, a Protestant now being in power, the Assembly was supernumerary and the authority it had temporarily enjoyed passed back to the godly prince — or in this case to his godly regent. It is understandable that the Assembly should hotly have contested this view and Morton had to resort to the introduction of a kind of bishop with a view to gaining supremacy in matters ecclesiastical. Thus in 1572 the Concordat of Leith restored bishops to the Kirk. There was no suggestion of introducing a full-blooded system of Episcopacy, much less of establishing a doctrine of Divine Right of Bishops. Indeed these were the so-called tulchan bishops — 'when a cow will not give her milk they stuff a calf's skin full of straw and set it down before her' — a tulchan. Make-believe or not, things were definitely moving in favour of the Crown.

But at this point there emerged on the scene one of the greatest figures in the history of the Scottish Kirk — Andrew Melville, whose main contribution was the Second Book of Discipline of 1581, setting the pattern of Presbyterianism as it continues to this day. Four years after Melville's return to Scotland, Morton resigned and the 12-year old king, assisted by his Council, took the reins of government into his own hand. It was clear that already in Melville's mind was a picture of a Kirk that would brook no bishop, where Church and State would be separate and distinct, the former being entitled to teach the civil magistrate how to exercise his jurisdiction according to the Word of God, and wherein the General Assembly (a court consisting of both ministers and elders representing the lower courts) would be vested with the fullest powers.

Thus there emerged in very vivid outline the true character of the issue that was confronting the nation. On the one side was a monarch who believed implicitly that he ruled by divine right, and that it was therefore his prerogative no less than his duty to prescribe the forms of creed, worship and discipline that should obtain within the Kirk just as he determined the form of law and government that obtained within the civil realm. On the other side was the Kirk, directed by men of the stamp of Andrew Melville who held that their creed, their worship, their discipline were to be founded upon the Word of God, that they themselves must be the sole judge of such conformity, that in matters of the faith they owed nothing to earthly rulers, that indeed it was the bounden duty of the monarch to maintain the Kirk in her freedom and to enforce her decrees. Both positions stemmed from the Reformation — the Divine Right of Kings being a direct consequence of the downgrading of the Papacy, the claim of the Kirk arising from her new faith in Christ as King. But however common their source, they were incompatible and there was bound to be trouble.

The essential contradiction between the two positions is nowhere more picturesquely highlighted than in the famous confrontation in Falkland Palace — 'Melville caught the king by the sleeve, calling him "but God's sillie vassal" and going on to declare, "Sir, as divers times before, so now again I must tell you, there are two kings and two kingdoms in Scotland: there is King James, the head of this commonwealth, and there is Christ Jesus and His Kingdom the Kirk, whose subject King James the Sixth is, and of whose kingdom not a king, nor a head, nor a lord but a member".' To James this was heresy, if not actually treason. He had a couthier principle — 'No bishop, no king' enshrined his philosophy, and from the teaching of Melville he turned to Episcopacy under which, through the bishops, it would be possible to manipulate the Church. 'The bishops must rule the ministers, and the king rule both.'

Thus in Scotland the opposition to the tyranny of an absolute rule based on the Divine Right of Kings was led by the Kirk. South of the border it was between King and Parliament that the contest raged. Kirk and Parliament were sufficiently close for them to unite forces in the Civil War, but the alliance was not strong enough to survive the defeat of the king.

For some time things had been going definitely the way of the Kirk and this reached its culmination in 1580 at Dundee when 'the whole Assembly of the Kirk in one voice found and declared the pretended office of a bishop to be unlawful, having neither foundation nor warrant in the Word of God, and ordained all such persons as brooked the said office to demit the same as an office to which they were not called by God, and to cease from preaching the Word and administering the Sacraments till they should be admitted anew by the General Assembly, under pain of excommunication'.

The Black Acts

It was only two years later, though, that there occurred the Raid of Ruthven when the king was held prisoner at

Huntingtower by Gowrie, aided by Marr, Glamis, and others, ostensibly to deliver and protect him from the malign influence of his favourites, Arran and Lennox. Once the king had escaped, the raid was declared treason; in May 1584 Gowrie was executed; and later that same month Parliament passed the Black Acts restoring Episcopacy under penal sanctions — first, the bishops were restored as members of the Three Estates; second, the king was declared supreme over all persons and to decline his jurisdiction was treason; third, all convocations not specifically licensed by the king were unlawful; fourth, the chief jurisdiction of the Church was to lie with the bishops; and fifth, there were to be no slanderous speeches, private or public, to the reproach of king or council. What must have seemed to the Kirk a merciful release came the following November when the banished lords entered Stirling Castle in force, met the king, and offered him a homage which may have saved his face but saved little else for him, for in reality he was capitulating to them.

Once James was really frightened concessions flew. In 1590 at the General Assembly he made a speech in extravagant praise of the Kirk, thanking God that it had been his good fortune to be king in such a Kirk, 'the sincerest Kirk in the world'. Tribute it may have been to the sincerity of the Kirk; it was no tribute to the sincerity of the king. Two years later (in 1592) the Assembly set out four articles in the form of a petition to the king and the following month Parliament passed an Act (sometimes referred to as the Magna Carta of the Kirk) which ratified its liberty, recognised the jurisdiction of its courts, abrogated the Black Acts of 1584, and ordained that presentations to parishes were to be directed not to bishops but to Presbyteries.

That particular round most certainly went to the Kirk — mistress in her own household, judge in her own cause.

James in London

The Kirk's triumph, however, was to be short-lived, and in 1596 there had begun the second main phase of the struggle, one that was to last till 1638.

Early in 1597 the king summoned an Assembly to meet at Perth at a time when the Convention of Estates had been deliberately summoned to meet there also. There were those who protested that it could not be a proper Assembly since it was not meeting on its own authority — their difficulty was met by calling it an extraordinary Assembly, which it certainly was! The king sent two commissioners, besides which he appeared in person and addressed the brethren on a number of occasions. Before rising the Assembly decreed to meet at Aberdeen the following year, but the king at his own hand changed time and place so that the Assembly met at Montrose in 1600 when it reluctantly agreed that certain ministers might vote in Parliament but expressly rejected the proposal that they should adopt the name of 'bishop'. This again was deliberately defied by the king who appointed three of his friends for the purpose and called them bishops.

In 1603, as we all know, James VI and I made his way to London to assume the crown of England. Three years later he summoned eight Scottish ministers (including Andrew and James Melville) to London to be 'reasoned with'. Since he proved obdurate as well as effective in the reasoning process Andrew Melville was clapped in the Tower where he languished for four years before going as Professor of Divinity to Sedan where he died in exile about 1622 — a pathetic end, surely, to the life of one of the ablest and most patriotic Scotsmen of all time. His brother was exiled to Newcastle, the other six being allowed to return to Scotland only under restriction. An unreasonable end, one might have thought, to a session of being reasoned with.

An even worse fate attended the commissioners to the Assembly held at Aberdeen in 1605, most of them ending up in ward in Blackness Castle on the Forth. The wheeling and dealing that had to be undertaken to secure verdicts against them by judges and juries who still had some lingering respect for justice is hard to credit.

In July of the following year (1606) Parliament confirmed the Royal Prerogative, declaring the monarch supreme over all persons and causes, as well as restoring the temporal estate of the bishops. Later that year, when the Kirk was weakened by the absence of more than a score of her ablest ministers — eight being reasoned with in London and 14 being in ward at Blackness — a convention of ministers summoned by royal missives agreed that the bishops should preside at all meetings within their bounds and that elsewhere there should be permanent moderators. In 1609 Parliament restored to the bishops still more of their erstwhile power and the following year a muzzled Assembly at Glasgow in effect re-established the whole system of Episcopacy. The opening days of the 17th century were ill days for the Kirk.

So things dreed their weird till 1618 when the Assembly at Perth passed the famous Five Articles. The Assembly had been called by the king; it was presided over by Archbishop Spottiswoode as of right; open discussion was not allowed; the Five Articles were dealt with on a single vote; and before that vote it was made clear that the names of everyone voting Against would be reported to the king. Yet, in spite of it all, 49 voted Against, as opposed to 83 who voted For.

To us today the Articles seem innocent enough — compulsory kneeling at communion, permission to celebrate communion privately, permission for private baptism, confirmation to be by bishops, and Christmas, Easter and other festivals of the Christian Year to be observed. One might think the opposition a storm in a teacup. Not so, for one has to bear in mind the atmosphere of the time when what had been a hatred of Rome and her customs was fast becoming a terror of Rome and her persecutions. In such circumstances the opposition is readily understandable — kneeling at communion spoke of transubstantiation, private communion with reserved elements was a form of idolatry, the celebration of Holy Days was not much better, confirmation by bishops was the thin edge of the Episcopal wedge. All of that apart, however, the opposition sprang from a conviction that all such matters should be left to the free decision of a General Assembly convened regularly in terms of the Kirk's own laws. It was all a clear case of Caesar meddling in the things that are God's, and as such it was not to be tolerated.

Three years later the Five Articles were ratified by Parliament, but even there in face of heavy opposition, the voting being 77 to 50 and the majority depending upon the votes of the bishops and higher nobility. Meantime the ordinary folk voted with their feet by staying away from those churches where the distasteful practices were being indulged in.

The year 1625 saw James succeeded on the throne by his son, Charles I.

The strange personality of King James had had a lot to do with shaping the unhappy events of these years. His bitter antipathy to the Kirk he owed in part to his favourites, Arran and Lennox, in part to his love of absolute power, in part in the early days to his prospect of the English throne, and in some part possibly to the over-strict discipline of his schooldays. Everyone knows Sully's description of him as 'the wisest fool in Christendom' but not so many perhaps are familiar with Macaulay's characterisation of him as 'made up of two men; a witty and well-read scholar who wrote, disputed, and harangued, and a nervous, drivelling idiot who acted'. If Margaret had been a sair saint for the Crown, James was a sair king for the Kirk.

Charles and Laud

Without doubt Charles I was a very much better man than his father. He was guided by principle and characterised by piety — and the most ardent admirer could not have said that of James! But while the father had a considerable skill in achieving his aim by guile the son had what amounted to a genius for doing the right thing in the wrong way; he had all the Stuart weakness for taking a heroic stand on an issue that mattered little while conceding the thing that was vital; he allowed himself to be influenced by the wrong people; he had been reared and educated in England and never got on to the Scottish wavelength. Would the Kirk fare better under a silly saint than it had under a silly scoundrel?

Two policies Charles took over direct from his father — that he would be an absolute monarch, and that he would bring the Kirk in Scotland into line with her southern neighbour, he himself to be head of both. Clearly he was set upon a multiple collision course — collision with an English Parliament that saw itself defending the democratic rights of the people, and collision with a Scottish Kirk committed to defend the Crown Rights of Christ. In 1633 the king, accompanied by his favourite Laud whom he had elevated to be Archbishop of Canterbury, paid a visit to Scotland, but for anything they learned of the Scots or of the Scottish outlook on religion they had as well stayed at home.

The king had the remarkably sound idea that if he could bring his two peoples into line in their pattern of worship most other things would fall into place. So the preparation of a Book of Common Prayer was put in hand, and had he pushed straight ahead with this project all might conceivably have been well. Instead of that he decided to prepare the way by a Book of Canons, and this he issued in 1636. Not only that, he had already fouled the pitch by restoring grants out of Kirk resources which his father had made to court favourites. Besides which, the Assembly had not met since 1618. So it was upon a highly suspicious Kirk that the Book of Canons was launched — with the Prayer Book still to come.

The very title of the volume is interesting — and challenging — 'Canons and Constitutions Ecclesiastical, gathered and put in form for the Government of the Church of Scotland. Ratified and approved by Authority, and ordered to be observed by the Clergy and all others whom they concern. Published by Authority.' Twice the word 'Authority' appears with a capital initial, but the title does not condescend upon whose authority. Not that of a General Assembly which had not met, nor that of a Parliament which had never heard of the book. Exclusively the authority of an absolute monarch — and an absolute fool.

One of the canons made it an offence entailing excommunication to say that the Book of Prayer contained anything repugnant to Scripture — yet the Book of Prayer was not completely prepared let alone published at this time. Other canons required for example that national or general assemblies were to be called by the king's authority, that no presbyter or reader was to offer extempore prayer under pain of deprivation, that no one was to be admitted to holy orders who did not subscribe these canons.

Was it any wonder the book received a bitterly hostile reception? Its object was clearly to deprive people of rights they had enjoyed for generations and to impose upon the Kirk a kind of oversight totally out of line with its history and utterly foreign to the character of its people.

The Book of Prayer

The Book of Canons having so effectively built up advance hostility, the Prayer Book when it appeared in 1637 with an order that it was to be used in all parish churches could expect a hot reception rather than a warm welcome. Nor were the expectations of trouble disappointed. It was the English Prayer Book carefully revised by Charles and Laud and it contained modifications by two of the Scottish bishops, these being principally in the direction of a more ritualistic observance of the Communion office. The Scots objections are perhaps best expressed in a petition prepared by Alexander Henderson of Leuchars for submission to the Privy Council:

> First because the book was warranted neither by the General Assembly nor by Act of Parliament: secondly because the liberties of the true Church, and the form of worship and religion received at the Reformation, and universally practised since were warranted by various Acts of Assembly and Acts of Parliament: thirdly because the Church of Scotland was a free and independent Church and its pastors were best able to provide what was for the good of the people: fourthly, because it was well known what disputes there had been over a few of the many ceremonies contained in that book which, when examined, would be found to depart from the established form of worship and to draw near to the anti-Christian Church of Rome: fifthly, because the people had always been taught a different doctrine, and would not agree to such changes, even if their pastors were willing to submit.

So, in convincing logical sequence, Henderson of Leuchars set forth the Kirk's reaction to the new book. It was in rather more violent fashion that Jenny Geddes, the herb-stall woman, gave voice to the popular response as she hurled her stool at the head of the celebrating clergyman in St Giles' with the words 'Villain, durst thou say mass in my lug?'. The ensuing riot set things moving as Henderson's petition had not done. There was a deal of correspondence with London, and early in 1638 the supporters of the cause of the freedom of the Kirk gathered in Edinburgh to put their names to the National Covenant.

The National Covenant

Considering the degree of provocation to which the people of Scotland had been subjected the National Covenant is a remarkably restrained and reasonable document. It had been prepared by a minister and a lawyer — Henderson of Leuchars and Johnston of Warriston who were later that year to become respectively Moderator and Clerk of the General

THE KIRK, THE CROWN

Assembly. It was divided into three parts — first a repetition of the King's Covenant (sometimes called the Negative Confession), that uncompromising rejection of Romanism prepared 50 years earlier and subscribed by James VI and I; second a list of the many Acts which the Scottish Parliament had passed against Romanism; and third a declaration of intent 'to recover the purity and liberty of the Gospel' and a prayer that 'religion and righteousness may flourish in the land to the glory of God, the honour of our king, and the peace and comfort of us all'. Here was nothing outrageous, certainly nothing treasonable — not at least on the face of it.

The Covenant was an instant success. The idea that men should bind themselves in a covenant had much going for it in Scotland where its Biblical roots commended it mightily. Great was the excitement in the Kirkyard of Greyfriars as the signing began. Soon the scenes were being re-enacted throughout the country. It was said that some signed in their own blood — some were going to have to ere long. Scotland was united as it has rarely been.

Was the Covenant as loyal as it sounded? What of its legality? As has been said, at face value it was above reproach. Its affirmation of loyalty to 'our dread sovereign the king's majestie, his person and authority' is quite touching. But it does not require much probing to recognise that the Covenant had one object and one object only — to band the people together against the king in his overweening ambition to be an absolute dictator. Situations arise in national history when nice questions of legality become irrelevant and the issue comes to be quite simply what is in the best interest of the people as a whole. As the historian Cook puts it, 'The vindication of the Covenant must be rested, not upon far-fetched attempts to reconcile it with loyalty, but upon this great principle that, when the ends for which all government should be instituted are defeated, the oppressed have a clear right to disregard customary forms, and to assert the privileges without which they would be condemned to the degradation and wretchedness of despotism.'[3] A nation convinced that there could be no true Kirk once it had been deprived of the power of self-determination had to take drastic steps to defend itself against a monarch who claimed that he had 'the same authority in causes ecclesiastical that the godly kings had among the Jews or the Church's emperors in the primitive Church', and who threatened excommunication to any who so much as doubted this. The signing of a Covenant was a modest enough reaction.

For once, it would seem, Charles I recognised just how serious was the position north of the border. So long as the Scots were bonded in this Covenant what was his authority worth? He would rather die, he declared, than submit to this kind of thing. In spite of these brave words he made an offer — he would cancel the Liturgy and the Canons, he would abolish the High Commission, he would suspend the Five Articles of Perth till approved by Assembly and Parliament, he would subscribe the King's Covenant, and he would pardon the past to all who agreed to act dutifully in future. It was too late. The Covenanting party had the bit between their teeth and were not prepared to consider any offer, however generous. Not that one could blame them, considering how fickle the word of a king had proved in times past. So they pressed ahead with arrangements for the Assembly.

The Assembly of 1638

It would be the first Assembly for 20 years and the first free Assembly for 30 years. Sadly it was not going to be a free Assembly, the difference being that this time it was not the king who was tampering with the works. The Tables sent secret instructions to Presbyteries regarding the election of representatives, the Presbytery of Edinburgh was cajoled into trumping up charges against the bishops since this would have the effect of sisting them at the bar and so prevent their sitting and voting as members. It was tragic that the Covenanting movement, established on so high a moral tone, should thus early have descended to the kind of skulduggery it had been designed to destroy.

It was in Glasgow Cathedral that the Assembly met on 21 November, and they spent most of the first week dealing with the constitution of the court. The Marquis of Hamilton was High Commissioner and when the Assembly moved on to the trial of the bishops he did all he could to stop them. It soon became clear that he could not prevail, so he dissolved the Assembly in the king's name and withdrew — accompanied by two elders and three ministers. The Assembly then proceeded to business in a really big way — they completely overthrew the Episcopal system, they rejected the recent innovations in worship, they restored elders to their place in the government of the Kirk. Unhappily, even if understandably, they showed that extreme intolerance that was later to besmirch the name of Covenanter by excommunicating some of the principal opponents of the Covenant.

On 20 December, a month after they had convened, the Assembly rose. According to one report the Moderator, in his closing address, said, 'We have now cast down the walls of Jericho, let him that rebuildeth them beware the curse of Hiel the Bethelite.' This seems unlikely to be true, though the words may have been spoken as an aside after the court had risen. Spoken or not, the words were apposite, for in consequence of the National Covenant and of the Assembly just concluded the Kirk was once again a free agent, mistress in her own household, judge in her own cause. It was not to be for long. The rebuilding of the walls of Jericho would soon be put in hand, and at the end of the day it would be hard to say on whom had fallen the curse of Hiel the Bethelite.

Only too tragically often it happens that one tyranny gives place to another, that those who have paid dearly to gain freedom will not extend it to others. So in this case the word 'Covenant' came very soon to stand for a new kind of oppression manifested principally in two phenomena. First there was the emergence of a strict puritanism quite foreign to Scotland. And secondly there was the Solemn League and Covenant of 1643, a document as much to be regretted as its predecessor had been to be welcomed. The National Covenant sought to bind Scots together in defence against having an alien English form of worship thrust upon them; the Solemn League and Covenant was an alliance with a minority party south of the border designed to impose a foreign Scottish pattern of worship upon the southern realm — and upon Ireland too for good measure.

Inevitably this new spirit led to division within the Covenanting ranks — on the one side the Protesters, 'up with the Covenants and down with the King', and on the other side the Resolutioners, broader in outlook and essentially loyalist at heart. The former party reached the peak of its influence with the Act of Classes of 1649 which drove out of public life all who were not dedicated to the Covenants. The Resolutioners, on the other hand, profited in a negative way from the beheading of the king, an event that utterly shocked Scottish public opinion, and for them it must have seemed a signal victory when in 1650 Charles II, having signed the Covenants, was crowned at Scone.

It took a new tyranny — that of Oliver Cromwell — to disband the General Assembly in 1653.

The Return of the Stuarts

And so we come to 1660, when the Stuarts returned and Episcopacy went into the ascendancy. The temper of the new reign was early and vividly expressed in three executions — first that of Argyll who ten years earlier at Scone had set the crown upon the royal brow; then that of James Guthrie, minister at Stirling, the short man who could not bow; and then that of Johnston of Warriston, Lord of Session, legal adviser to the Kirk on many issues, who had acted as Clerk to the 1638 Assembly.

The new king began with sweet words, however. In August 1660 he addressed a letter to the Presbytery of Edinburgh in which he said, 'We do also resolve to protect and preserve the government of the Church of Scotland as it is settled by law, without violation, and to countenance, in the due exercise of their functions, all such ministers as shall behave themselves dutifully and peaceably as becomes men of their calling'. He went on to promise a General Assembly 'as soon as our affairs shall permit'. Considering that Charles II was at this point utterly committed to a policy of asserting his own authority over all persons and in all causes it is hard to see why he should have gone out of his way to introduce himself to the Kirk as a liar and a cheat.

In March 1661 Parliament passed the Act Rescissory which rescinded all Church legislation subsequent to 1640, thus taking the position back to that of 1633 with the king supreme over all persons and in all causes. This was followed in May 1662 by an Act for the Restitution and Re-establishment of the Ancient Government of the Church by Archbishops and Bishops. About the same time the signing of the Covenants was declared treasonable and the National

Covenant was burned in dishonour at Linlithgow, the very document to which the king had been so quick to put his name twelve years before. A further Act of that same year required all ministers if they were to remain in office to secure fresh presentation from the patron and institution from the bishop. Nearly 300 left home and parish rather than submit to this indignity.

This was what gave rise to the conventicle, the field preaching. After all, 300 parishes had at one blow been deprived of their ministers, most of them men greatly loved. And what had been put in their place? Not a Covenanting source but Bishop Gilbert Burnet said: 'They were generally very mean and despicable in all respects, the worst preachers I have ever heard, ignorant to a reproach, and many of them openly vicious. They were a disgrace to their order, and were indeed the dregs and refuse of the northern parts. Those of them who were above contempt or scandal were men of such violent tempers that they were as much hated as the others were despised.' To all of which has to be added that in the darkest days of persecution many of them were diligent to act as spies and informers against their Presbyterian parishioners.

It was not to be wondered at, then, that men and women should take to the moors to worship with the man they still looked upon as their own minister. An innocent enough reaction, you might think. Yet the government retaliated with incredible brutality. In 1670 an Act was passed whereby a field preacher could be punished with death; another made criminal every baptism conducted; yet another made it an offence to be absent from Church on three successive Sundays. This Act was nicknamed the Bishop's Dragnet and, believe it or not, each Sunday at the close of service the roll was called and the persistent absentees were reported by the curate to the commander of the nearest troop of dragoons. Varied are the ways of attracting a good congregation! In 1678 the Highland Host descended upon the south-west, bringing desolation in their train. The murder of Archbishop Sharpe by a group of outlawed Covenanters in the following year did nothing to advance their cause. The Covenanting victory at Drumclog was quickly followed by Bothwell Brig when defeat was the only possible outcome of that awful weakness of their cause, the complete impossibility to reach a common mind on any subject since each group was utterly convinced that their view was the *ipse dixit* of the Almighty. They were to pay dearly for it.

While these measures were being taken against the more belligerent of the followers of the Covenants a series of indulgences was introduced, creating, naturally, more divisions. The first in 1669 permitted a peaceable ousted minister to hold manse, glebe and a yearly 'maintenance' on condition that he ministered only within his own parish. Forty-three of the ejected ministers were attracted back. A second indulgence three years later was accepted by 80 more. The tragedy of all this was that it set the Covenanters even more bitterly one against the other since those who could not see their way to accept the indulgences labelled those who did as backsliders, cowards and traitors, men who had contracted out of the fellowship of the true Kirk — an attitude well illustrated in the fact that when after the Revolution Settlement all had returned those who had stayed out until then set themselves up as the true Presbyteries, ignoring those who had acceded sooner.

One cannot view the conventicle with other than admiration. These were no treasonable gatherings but groups of decent peace-loving citizens meeting to worship God in a way that was meaningful and dear to them, to do homage to God even if the *diktat* of a power-hungry sovereign had declared it illegal so to do. In many ways this is a glorious page of Scottish history — though it may not be such a glorious page of Church history. For the unfortunate thing is that it was this period of the conventicle that sowed the seed from which sprang the idea that the Church takes second place to the individual believer, the doctrine that in all matters of faith it is personal conviction that alone is of consequence, so that the individual must be sole judge — my conscience against the world.

It is said that during this period of acute persecution someone in derision asked a Covenanter, 'Where is your Church of Scotland now?'. To which came the instant response, 'Show me a man prayin' ahint a dyke an' I'll show you the Kirk in Scotland today'. As a debating point it is excellent: but is it meaningful? The sight of a man praying ahint a dyke is indeed an impressive one. Loud and clear it speaks of deep personal conviction, of an intense individual faith, but it is not in any sense a picture of a Kirk. It was sad indeed that in Scotland — probably just because the Scot is the individualist that he is — the result of these years of persecution was not to bind people together for mutual preservation, but to set them at enmity one with another; sad indeed if the result of men being driven to pray ahint dykes was to convince them there could be no better place to pray, that united witness was of no great concern, that the Communion of Saints was no greater than one's own ability to conceive it.

After Bothwell Brig

The vengeance wreaked after Bothwell Brig was indeed terrible. So terrible as to drive the extremists to yet sterner courses and to make those who had accepted indulgence wonder whether they could continue in so unholy an alliance. Matters were brought to a head in 1680 when Richard Cameron nailed his theses to the market cross at Sanquhar:

> We do by these presents disown Charles Stuart that has been reigning, or rather tyrannising, over Britain these years bygone, as having any right, title to, or interest in, the crown of Scotland, for government — as forfeited several years since by his perjury and breach of covenant both to God and His Kirk and by his tyranny and breach of the essential conditions of government in matters civil...: We do declare war with such a usurper, and all men of his practices.... And we hope that after this none will blame us for, or offend at, our rewarding those that are against us as they have done to us, as the Lord gives us opportunity.

It was only a few months later that Cameron with a handful of supporters was surprised at Aird's Moss and died in the engagement that followed. But his name lived on.

Later, in the autumn of that same year, at Torwood near Larbert, Donald Cargill, who had been deprived of his charge of The Barony in Glasgow, and who had been with Cameron at Sanquhar solemnly excommunicated the King, the Duke of York, and five others. In recognition of this service the reward of 3000 merks that had been put upon his head was increased to 5000, and, on his being betrayed at Covington

Mill the following year, he was executed with four others at the Cross of Edinburgh.

So things went on. In 1681 there was passed the Test Act, what chemists would call 'the mixture as before'. Everyone in public life had to swear that he owned the true Protestant religion as explained in the Confession of 1567; that he acknowledged the king to be supreme in all causes and over all persons both civil and ecclesiastical; that he would never consult about any matter of state without His Majesty's express licence and command; and never endeavour any alteration in the government of the country. Nearly 80 ministers left their parishes rather than forswear themselves. The issue in 1685 of a new Proscription List containing 2000 names was mercifully followed by the death of the king before any action could be taken to make it effective.

The accession of the Duke of York as King James VII brought a measure of relief, not because the new sovereign loved the Kirk any more dearly than had his predecessors, but merely because some of the legislation which he introduced in the attempt to win the country back to the allegiance of Rome had the side-effect of easing the pressure on Presbyterians. In 1687 the king, without consent of Parliament, passed an Act of Toleration — directed, needless to say, in favour of Rome — but in such terms that a great many of the more moderate Presbyterians were able to avail themselves of it. The Cameronians, though, scorned all favours. Their chief preacher at this time, James Renwick, was to be the last of the martyrs.

It was Renwick who, at this point, was leader of what remained of the Covenanters, and we may read with interest his own words describing the company he headed — 'a poor, wasted, wounded, afflicted, bleeding, misrepresented and reproached Remnant and Handful of suffering people who desire to throw down what God will throw down, and to build what He will establish when He comes — to whom be the Kingdom and the Dominion for ever and ever'. It rings with the same note of finality and authority as does 'shall be sole judge'. It was against this young man of 25 that the whole fury of the government was now directed. Some idea of the affection in which he was held by the powers-that-be is to be gauged from the following edict of the Privy Council which 'commands and charges all and sundry our lieges and subjects that they nor none of them presume nor take upon hand to reset, supply, or intercommune with the said Mr James Renwick, rebel aforesaid, nor furnish him with meat, drink, house, harbour, victual, or other things useful or comfortable to him; or to have intelligence with him by word writ or message or any other way or manner whatsoever, on the pain of being esteemed art and part with him in the crimes foresaid ...'. They surely did not wish him well! After a number of hairbreadth escapes, including an occasion when he stood at the stirrup of the officer who was directing the search for him, Renwick was taken in Edinburgh early in 1688 and hanged there on 17 February, the last of the martyrs — a company believed to have numbered as many as 18 000.

Revolution Settlement

Then came the flight of King James, the accession of William and Mary, and, in 1690, the Revolution Settlement. Episcopacy was set aside, the Presbyterian system of 1592 was revived, the ousted ministers were restored, the first meeting of the General Assembly for 37 years was called, and the claim of the Stuarts that the king should be supreme in every sphere was finally repudiated. It is important to note, considering the spirit of the age, that no claim was made that Presbyterianism was the only true form of the faith — what was averred was that it was the form of the faith acceptable to most of the people of Scotland and that it was 'agreeable to the Word of God'. To the grief of the extremists there was no mention of the Covenants. But, Covenant or no Covenant, the Kirk was now, as the old banns notice used to say, 'fully and finally' declared to be mistress in her own household, judge in her own cause.

We may sum up the results of all these years in three sentences. First, in its bitter, unrelenting hostility to episcopacy the Kirk was not contending against a rival system of Church government but was resisting the introduction of a structure which would put into the hands of the sovereign through the ecclesiastical hierarchy that power which properly belongs to the Kirk itself — it was not for Presbytery it was fighting but for the Crown Rights of Christ. Second, while in the circumstances of the time the National Covenant had an enormous influence for good, its long-term effects were fragmentation, schism and bitterness, so that when the time came for the Kirk to be mistress in her own household the comment could well have been made, 'But what a household'! And third, the experience of the conventicle and of managing well enough without recourse to an establishment greatly diminished the influence of the Church and made it only too easy to elevate the individual conscience to a quite terrifying height.

References
1 Mechie, Stewart. (1957). *The Office of Lord High Commissioner*. The Saint Andrew Press, Edinburgh, Foreword vii.
2 General Assembly Reports for 1984, p183ff.
3 Cook, George. (1815). *The History of the Church of Scotland*. Edinburgh, II, p415.

III

Kirk Creed and Christian Conscience

The Bar of Conscience
What is the difference between conscience and conviction? How do you distinguish between my believing something to be true because my conscience tells me so and my believing something to be true because I have become utterly convinced that it is so? There is a short answer which it is tempting to offer: the difference is that while you can argue with conviction there is no arguing with conscience. You can try by a process of reasoning to show a man that his conviction is wrong, that he is starting from false evidence, that his conclusions are logically invalid, that he has not taken all the relevant considerations into his calculation, and so on. You may even be successful in persuading him of his error. But you cannot argue with conscience, for conscience is the voice of the Holy Spirit, and the Holy Spirit does not enter the debating chamber. To anyone who like myself enjoys a good argument it is galling when hot in pursuit of your opponent you see him going to earth with an appeal to conscience. I remember on an occasion when I was involved in the ecumenical debate my Anglican counterpart saying, 'Of course you prefer Presbyterianism, it's only natural that you should, but for us, don't you see, the historic episcopate is a matter of conscience.' Where do you go from there? 'Home' I suppose is the only answer.

You remember the verse from Browning's *Rabbi Ben Ezra* —

> Now, who shall arbitrate?
> Ten men love what I hate,
> Shun what I follow, slight what I receive,
> Ten who in ears and eyes
> Match me: we all surmise
> They this thing and I that: whom shall my soul believe?

Yes, who shall arbitrate, who shall be sole judge? Browning

puts the question very sharply — whom shall my soul believe? It is unfortunate that he does not even suggest an answer.

When considerations of conscience enter into any cause the owner of the conscience can be counted upon to set himself up as sole judge in that cause. From the bar of his conscience there can be no appeal.

The relevance of all of this will become apparent as we proceed.

We saw in the last chapter how after more than a century of struggle the Kirk triumphed over the Crown in the establishment of her autonomy. The next challenge to the Kirk's authority came from within her own ranks, from the conscience of the individual Churchman — though, as I have hinted in my opening observations, it is not always easy to know precisely what that means.

But first we must go back, not just back to where we left off, but earlier than that; for we must look somewhat narrowly at two events which in our whistle-stop trip from the Reformation to the Revolution we did not mention. They fell within the period covered but were not germane to the matter then in hand. Both are, however, highly relevant to our theme in this chapter. They were the calling of the Westminster Assembly in 1643 and the abolition of patronage in 1690.

The Westminster Assembly

Without doubt the most lasting, and probably the most significant, outcome of the Solemn League and Covenant was the appointment of the Westminster Assembly which began its sessions in the Jerusalem Chamber in Westminster Abbey in July 1643, continuing through five years. The Assembly had been constituted by an ordinance of the Lords and Commons of England dated 12 June 1643 and had been given the remit 'that such a government should be settled in the Church as may be most agreeable to God's Holy Word, and most apt to produce and preserve the peace of the Church at home, and nearer agreement with the Church of Scotland and other Reformed Churches abroad'. The body to which this ambitious task was committed consisted of ten peers, 20 members of Commons, and 121 clergymen chosen by Parliament (the Long Parliament) and reflecting the religious complexion of that body — Congregationalists, Baptists, Episcopalians, but principally Presbyterian Puritans. Before it had time to meet, though, the Assembly was declared illegal by order of the king, and it was only 69 of the commissioners who, in defiance of the royal displeasure, were prepared to take part. Naturally enough it was those with Episcopal leanings who were filtered out at this juncture and the Assembly in consequence gained an overwhelming Presbyterian and Independent majority. The Scots were invited to attend the discussions, and in fact sent assessors headed by Alexander Henderson and including men of the stamp of Baillie, Rutherford and Johnston of Warriston. In the debating this group exerted no little influence — after all, they were the people who knew something about that Presbyterianism which was the subject under discussion.

It is important to recognise that the Westminster Assembly was never any more than an advisory body, that it possessed no authority whatever. All its recommendations had to be laid before Parliament and by that body accepted or rejected. Obviously this was an Erastian position representing the denial of everything for which Scottish Presbyterianism stood and for which at this time it was battling so bravely. It is not to be wondered at if the English Parliament had little inclination to set up in their midst a Church with the claims to autonomy they had seen in the north — that would indeed have been to shape a stick to beat their own back. Congregationalists and Baptists were equally unhappy at the thought of the establishment in the country of a Presbyterianism likely to oppress them every bit as heavily as Episcopacy had done. In consequence, little progress was made towards implementing the terms of the Solemn League and Covenant to the extent of settling the government of the Church in England on the Presbyterian model. Progress was made, however, in other directions — with the production of a *Directory of Public Worship*, a *Confession of Faith*, a *Larger and a Shorter Catechism*, and a *Book of Metrical Psalms*, and these had a deep and ongoing effect, not in England for which they were ostensibly intended, but north of the border, and, in the case of the Confession, throughout the world.

Inevitably the Westminster Confession will be referred to below again — and again. The point to be made at this stage is that when under the Revolution Settlement Presbyterianism was finally established in Scotland what precisely was adopted was Presbyterianism according to Andrew Melville (as that had been enshrined in the Act of 1592), with this change that in place of Knox's *Scots Confession* there was substituted *The Westminster Confession*. And the reason for that was that in its enthusiasm for the new Presbyterianism that was being hammered out at Westminster and soon to obtain throughout the British Isles, the Scots accepted the new confession without question; not only so, they accepted the new *Directory of Public Worship* and the *Book of Metrical Psalms*, so that these were in regular use in Scotland in Stuart times. And if the Confession was to be accepted what more natural than the acceptance of the two Catechisms that were explanatory thereof. By a strange quirk of fate, therefore, as Professor McEwen points out, 'Scottish Presbyterian standards in worship, faith, and even psalmody are to this day those that were authorised by a somewhat Erastian English Parliament in the mid-17th century'.[1]

Abolition of Patronage

In every Scottish parish the landowners, the heritors, were under obligation to build and maintain a church and a manse, to provide a glebe, and to pay a stipend. It was not unnatural — some would have thought it reasonable — that they should expect a large say in choosing who was to live in the manse and enjoy the stipend. The principal heritor in fact enjoyed the right of patronage, the right to present the living to whom he would, though in this connection there are two things to be borne in mind — first that before the presentee could be inducted the Presbytery had to take him on trials and satisfy itself as to the adequacy of his qualifications, and secondly that while the patron had the right to hire he had no power to fire — once the presentee had been inducted to the parish all the benefits, spiritual and temporal, vested in him, and this link could be broken only by the Presbytery. Induction was *ad vitam aut culpam*, and the power of the patron ended with presentation. This state of affairs had continued without challenge for a very long time, though there had been a short break between 1640 and 1661 when the right was temporarily abolished.

By the time of the Revolution Settlement, however, the operation of patronage was giving great offence. A spirit of democracy was in the air. Long and hard the Kirk had fought to be mistress in her own household, yet here when it came to a choice of supreme importance to the whole household it was a rank outsider who stepped in and said what was to be. Pressure was therefore brought to bear to have patronage abolished once and for all. King William, it would seem, had grave reservations — but the Jacobite threat was at such a pitch he could not afford to imperil Presbyterian support, so an Act was passed providing that in all vacancies the heritors and elders were to nominate a person for the approval of the congregation. The congregation were to have the right to disapprove, but if they did so they must state their reasons which would be finally adjudged by the Presbytery. By way of reparation for being deprived of their ancient right the heritors in each case were to receive from the parishioners the sum of 600 merks in return for which they were to give a formal Note of Renunciation. The new system came into operation without any insistence on the compensation being paid, so that 20 years later it was found that of all the parishes in Scotland only the two Monklands were in the clear, though Calder and Strathblane claimed to have paid though not to have received the formal Renunciation.

Restoration of Patronage
So with the Revolution Settlement Scotland happily bade farewell to patronage. But only for a season, a season that was to last for just 22 years, and 1712 saw the Parliament of the recently united kingdoms put the law of patronage back on the statute-book. There can be no doubt the motives were purely political, and the Act represented an unashamed encroachment by the State on what would generally be conceded to be the proper domain of the Kirk — the settlement of ministers in parishes.

It was a day when the question of the succession to the throne was becoming an urgent one. It was well known that the Tory administration was in favour of a return of the Stuarts and it was believed that Queen Anne herself would have been happy to think that she would be succeeded by her brother. It was in this atmosphere that the Toleration Act of

1711 by repealing the penal laws against them allowed the Episcopalians to celebrate their religious rites in freedom. The Act was a reasonable one, long overdue in fact, and it was unfortunate that it should have been popularly regarded (not perhaps without reason) as part of a deep-laid Jacobite plot. The same was true of the Patronage Act of the following year. A great many of the patrons were Episcopal — in sympathy if not in practice — and the Act, cleverly handled, could secure a preponderance of Episcopal opinion within the Kirk, thus facilitating a Stuart return. One thing was certain — such a return would bode ill for Presbyterian Church government in Scotland.

While suspicion of unworthy motives there might be, it was not difficult to advance a strong case in favour of a return of patronage. As noted earlier only four parishes had paid the 600 merks and this seemed to indicate the others did not set a great value on the right of choice; there had been unfortunate instances of how badly the new regulations could work; and, when all was said and done, the obligations which the heritors carried surely conferred upon them some compensating advantage. An unsuccessful attempt had been made to have stipends increased — 'Are we supposed to pay still more and to get still less?' the petulant heritors enquired. In any case the parishioners were not suffering. The existing practice gave them no right of unlimited choice but only the right to object to a nominee on reason stated — they were to have the identical right to object to a presentee. The Act was duly passed. Year after year the Assembly went through the motions of protesting against it.

Increasingly what happened was that the patron — often the crown or the burgh or a university — did not make a presentation, and as a result of the operation of the *ius devolutum* it fell, after six months, to the Presbytery to make an appointment. The practice of Presbyteries in such cases varied considerably. So in 1731 an Overture was approved by Assembly and sent down under Barrier Act providing that when an appointment fell to Presbytery it should be made upon a call from those heritors who were Protestant along with the elders, any member of the congregation having the right to object, and the Presbytery being judge of the force of such objection. It was not an attempt to get rid of patronage

KIRK CREED AND CHRISTIAN CONSCIENCE 53

but merely to tidy up the procedure to be followed when the patron's rights were not being enforced.

But it was the conversion of this modest Overture into an Act by the Assembly of 1732 that aroused the awful wrath of Ebenezer Erskine and that led 21 months later to the first secession from the Kirk.

Ebenezer Erskine

Born at Dryburgh in 1680 of a family that had known persecution as Covenanters, Ebenezer Erskine became minister at Portmoak on Loch Leven where he remained for 28 years before moving to Stirling. He was a most effective preacher, his favourite theme being the free grace offered in Christ. It has been said of him that he was 'a dignified type, intense and conscientious, righteous and devout, judging sternly, not broad-minded, but a man of strong conviction and a determined leader'.[2]

From his place in the Assembly Erskine had bitterly attacked the Overture when it was being debated there. On the Sunday after the Act was passed he no less bitterly denounced it from his pulpit in Stirling though by then, of course, it was the law of the Kirk. He was due to take the chair as Moderator of Synod at the autumn meeting of that court and therefore to preach at the opening service in St John's Kirk in Perth. He availed himself of the occasion to make an even more vitriolic attack — just how extreme may be gauged from the closing peroration:

> An Act is passed by the Assembly confining the power of election unto heritors and elders, whereby a new wound is given to the prerogative of Christ and the privileges of His subjects. I shall say the less of this Act now, that I had the opportunity to exoner myself with relation to it before the National Assembly where it was passed. Only allow me to say, that whatever Church authority may be in that Act, yet it wants the authority of the Son of God. All ecclesiastical authority under heaven is derived from Him, and therefore any Act that wants His authority has no authority at all. And seeing the reverend Synod has put me in this place where I am in Christ's stead, I must be allowed to say of this Act what I apprehend Christ Himself would say of it were He personally present where I am; that is, that by this Act the corner-

stone is receded from: He is rejected in his poor members, and the rich of this world put in their room. If Christ were personally present where I am by the Synod's appointment in His stead, He would say in reference to that Act, 'Inasmuch as ye have done it to one of the least of these little ones ye did it to me'.

Reaction to Sermon

One's first reaction on hearing an outburst of this kind must be one of horror at the spiritual arrogance — if not actual profanity — of a preacher who presumes to tell us what Christ Himself would have said had He been there in person — such a man must indeed see himself as far ben in the counsels of the Almighty. In the second place one must wonder how Erskine could reconcile such an attack on a decision taken after due process of law by the highest court of the Church with his ordination vow that he would make himself subject to the Presbytery and to the superior courts of the Church. Third, one wonders what was his conception of democracy. On his own showing he had taken full advantage of his opportunity to oppose the measure. Could not the majority claim they were following the leading of the Holy Spirit? Fourth, one might think it a cowardly thing to fulminate in this way from a pulpit when none could speak back. And last, one feels that he must have been peculiarly ignorant of the structure of Church courts if he genuinely thought that the Synod appointed a Moderator to stand before it as the representative of Christ and to address it as His mouthpiece. The business of a Moderator is to keep good order, and each solitary member of the court enjoys an equal title to claim that he is interpreting the mind of Christ. A diatribe of the sort quoted is the kind of thing of which one hopes the author, once he has had time to cool off and take a fresh look at things and regain some sense of proportion, will feel thoroughly and heartily ashamed.

It is possible that if Erskine had been allowed a sufficient cooling-off period things might have been different. What actually happened was that when the Synod met for the despatch of business one member claimed that the Moderator had said some things that were offensive to the brethren, and a committee was appointed which later reported there were passages in the sermon which were disrespectful to the

Assembly. After a long discussion — three days long — it was resolved by a majority of six that the preacher should be censured. Against this sentence Erskine appealed to the Assembly.

At the Assembly of 1733 Erskine appeared, supported now by three friends, Wilson of Perth, Moncrieff of Abernethy, and Fisher of Kinclaven. He read a paper in which he made the claim that he was bound to say what he did, a claim which, however startling, has to be taken very seriously, for it is an expression of the doctrine that my allegiance to my Kirk must take second place to my allegiance to my conscience. By comparison his other plea seems rather ridiculous — that there was nothing in the Act to say that you must not preach against it. The Assembly found that parts of the sermon were 'offensive and calculated to disturb the peace and good order of the Church' and that the author should be rebuked at the bar. Once again the affair might have ended there. But in anticipation of such a conclusion Erskine had prepared a paper, signed also by his friends, and this they laid on the table as they left the court. Although the paper was a highly discourteous document they flatly refused to withdraw it. The Assembly, it would seem, were unwilling to press the matter, but on the other hand they could not simply ignore what amounted to contempt — contempt persisted in at that. A cooling-off period seemed called for, so they remitted the case to the August Commission which was to suspend the ministers if they were still obdurate, and the November Commission was to proceed to a higher censure if the suspension was not obeyed.

A fair amount of sympathy was now developing in Erskine's favour, the original incident being seen as little more than an indiscretion. A molehill was becoming a mountain. So memorials were submitted to the Commission to the effect that Erskine had already suffered enough. Seen from this distance in time, it is hard to believe that it was just an indiscretion. The sermon did not just throw down a challenge to the courts of the Church, it completely and utterly denied that the courts of the Kirk had any power in face of a man whose conscience dictated otherwise. A Kirk that claimed to be sole judge in all matters ecclesiastical simply had to take note of so patent an affront.

Erskine Suspended

When the August Commission came round the four recusants appeared, but not in the least cooled-off. Erskine was allowed to read a paper which so far from expressing contrition hurled defiance. The Commission had no alternative but to obey its orders and suspend all four from the exercise of their ministerial functions. Came November and the four appeared at the bar to announce that they had deliberately flouted the sentence, having preached and administered the sacraments as usual. Even in face of this affront the Commission hesitated to proceed. A plea for further delay was defeated on the casting vote of the Moderator. Yet a further attempt was made to achieve a modified withdrawal, but when this proved abortive the Commission passed sentence, severing the pastoral tie that bound the four ministers to their congregations and declaring them to be no longer ministers of the Church of Scotland.

To some it seemed a needlessly stern sentence; to others it may well have appeared that when Erskine preached his Synod sermon he was declaring himself to be no longer a minister of the Church of Scotland.

Before leaving the Commission the four protested that the finding would in no way affect their relationship with their congregations, nor indeed with those of their brethren who had not 'given way to the defection of the time'. The prevailing party in the Church, they maintained, had declined from covenanted principles, had suppressed ministerial freedom, and had expelled them from their fellowship. They went on:

> Therefore, we do, for these and many other weighty reasons to be laid open in due time, protest that we are obliged to make a secession from them, and that we can have no ministerial communion with them till they see their sins and mistakes and amend them. And in like manner we do protest that it shall be lawful and warrantable for us to exercise the keys of doctrine, discipline and government according to the Word of God and the Confession of Faith, and the principles and constitutions of the covenanted Church of Scotland, as if no such censure had been passed upon us; upon all which we take instruments. And we hereby appeal to the first free, faithful and reforming General Assembly of the Church of Scotland.

The First Secession

As is well known, on 5 December of that same year (1733) the four, who had now been joined by Ralph Erskine of Dunfermline, Ebenezer's younger brother, met at Gairney Bridge near Kinross, and, after consultation and solemn prayer, constituted themselves the Associate Prebytery. This was later to become the Associate Synod, and later still the Secession Church. Thus begins a new chapter in Church history.

The previous chapter, however, cannot be properly concluded until the severance between the seceders and the Kirk had been made complete. No sooner had sentence been passed than the Synod began to suffer from second thoughts and approaches were made to the General Assembly which apparently shared these second thoughts and which now proceeded to what might seem incredible lengths to achieve reconciliation. They withdrew the Act which had given offence in the first place; they found in effect that ministerial freedom was to be interpreted as allowing unlimited criticism of the activities of the courts; they empowered the Synod of Perth to accept the four if they should apply for restoration; and they took every step competent to them to have patronage abolished. It seems strange that the ruling party in the Kirk should not have recognised a parting of the ways when they met one.

Predictably Erskine and company were not to be appeased. For a long time, he said, he had been swimming against the current within the Kirk. 'There is a difference to be made between the Established Church of Scotland and the Church of Christ in Scotland, for I reckon that the latter is in great measure driven into the wilderness by the first. And since God in His adorable providence has led us into the wilderness with her, I judge it to be our duty to tarry with her for a while there, and to prefer her afflictions to all the advantages of a legal establishment.' In 1736 the group published their Judicial Testimony, a document about which I shall have a word to say later. Clearly Erskine had never learned to pray for grace to believe that the other fellow might just conceivably be right — or if he had, his prayer had not been answered.

Matters were allowed to drag on, with repeated efforts to

effect reconciliation and bring the defectors back into the fold. Not only were these unsuccessful, but also disorderly situations were arising. Dunfermline was a collegiate charge, so Ralph Erskine would fulminate against the establishment on a Sunday morning while his colleague would defend it in the afternoon — not very edifying even if highly entertaining. Ebenezer barred five of his elders from the Kirk Session because they could not accept Secession principles, and then went so far as to summon them from the pulpit 'to appear before the judgment-seat of Christ on the day appointed in God's decree'. Identifying himself with Christ seems to have become something of a habit with the leader of the Secession.

After still more appeals had fallen upon deaf ears, the Assembly of 1740 decided that enough was enough and by a very large majority resolved to depose the five ministers. For eight years they had remained in their manses and drawn their stipends while spreading discontent and disaffection throughout the Kirk. And that apparently without any scruple of conscience.

Theological Considerations
As already suggested, it is tempting to see the Secession as having its origin in hostility to patronage, to view it as a protest against 'having respect to the man with the gold ring and the gay clothing beyond the man with the vile raiment and the poor attire' as Erskine himself so colourfully expressed it. But the explosion while it was sparked off by the issue of patronage certainly drew all its force from the clash between the claims of the creed laid down by the Kirk as Kirk and the conscientious conviction of the Christian as an individual believer. Erskine's behaviour subsequent to the Synod sermon was directed not against patronage but against those who would have him accept a judgment regularly reached in the courts so long as it ran contrary to a conviction conscientiously held in his own heart. There had been other forces at work to produce this acute consciousness of conscience — as he himself said, he had been swimming against the current in the Kirk for a long time.

In an attempt to understand this allusion we shall pick up the thread left dangling near the start of this chapter — the Westminster Confession of Faith. The Revolution Settlement

KIRK CREED AND CHRISTIAN CONSCIENCE

had designed the Westminster Confession as 'the public and avowed confession of this Church, containing the sum and substance of the doctrine of the Reformed Churches'. The Toleration Act of 1711, however, set aside this formula, replacing it with a much tighter personal commitment — 'I sincerely own and believe the whole doctrine contained in the Confession of Faith ... to be the truth of God; and I do own the same as the Confession of my own Faith.' A subtle but significant change had been effected. What had been a declaration of where the Kirk stood had now become the personal profession of where the individual stood. The Kirk was becoming equipped for the heresy hunt.

It was three years after this that the Assembly was asked to enquire into the teaching of Mr John Simson, Professor of Divinity at Glasgow University, who, it was alleged, was spreading heretical doctrines. The Assembly declined to deal with the matter on the ground that the proper procedure was for the Presbytery of Glasgow to institute a libel. This was done, but the affair came back to the Assembly in 1716 and a committee was appointed to make enquiries. Two years later the committee reported, suggesting in effect that Simson might well be guilty of Arminianism. The Assembly did not find the charge proven, but they found that Simson had used expressions capable of misinterpretation and they warned him to be more careful in future. This enormously annoyed the strict Calvinists who thought sterner measures should be taken, and wanted to see an example made.

The situation was aggravated by an odd series of events in the Presbytery of Auchterarder. That body apparently felt that the questions prescribed to be put at licence were not of fine enough mesh to catch heretics, of whom there were many around, so they devised six additional questions of their own, and as a result of the operation of these refused an extract of licence to a Mr Craig who took the matter by appeal to the General Assembly. One of the questions was clearly capable of bearing two interpretations, and the document, derisively called 'The Auchterarder Creed', was condemned by the Assembly. Here was fresh fuel for the Calvinist fire: a court of the Church rebuked because it made an honest attempt to maintain the purity of the faith against the Simsons of the Universities. It is illuminating to read McKerrow, historian of the Secession — 'The tenderness shown to Professor Simson contrasted with the severe treatment of a Presbytery which had evinced its zeal for evangelical doctrine, filled many good men with ominous apprehensions as to the state of religious belief among the ministers of the Church.'[3]

It was as far back as 1645 that there had appeared a book from the pen of an English Puritan called *The Marrow of Modern Divinity*. About the turn of the century Thomas Boston came upon a copy and found its doctrine of grace to be most satisfying. This doctrine of grace was certainly in line with that of the Auchterarder Creed, and in 1720 the book was condemned by the General Assembly. The following year 12 ministers (including the two Erskines) signed a 'representation' against this decision. For this the Assembly of 1722 censured them and they protested. Without wishing to enter into the 'Marrow Controversy' let me say that the book stressed the importance in religion of feeling, of conscience, of nearness to God as against reason and good conduct. The matter is important from our point of view as showing Ebenezer, ten years before the patronage issue, at loggerheads with the Assembly over the right of the individual to follow his conscience and protest rather than accept the decisions of the Kirk. In other respects, strangely enough, he seemed to think that the creed of the Kirk must be supreme — the Simsons of this world were to keep their consciences to themselves.

It is this persecuting attitude — a heritage one feels from the Covenanters — which comes through so strongly in the Judicial Testimony, published in 1736 by the seceding group. The Covenants are declared to be binding not only upon those who signed them but upon their children and children's children; Protesters and Remonstrants are lauded and the craven time-servers who accepted indulgences are condemned; complaint is made that Episcopacy (which is called prelacy) was merely set aside in favour of Presbytery in 1690 when it should have been declaimed an accursed thing contrary to the Word of God; Episcopal hirelings were being allowed to continue in their parishes; union had been effected between the two kingdoms but not in terms of the Solemn League and Covenant; there was heresy in Divinity chairs, but the offending professor had not been excommunicated nor even deposed; balls and night assemblies were taking place; the penal statutes against witches had been repealed; and so on. Not much Christian charity in evidence here, not much consideration for the tender conscience of the other chap, not a plea that a place should be found in the creed of the Kirk for the conscientious scruple, but rather a plea that a creed should be framed that was conformable to my conscience even if to no other, and that it should be rigorously imposed.

The Judicial Testimony is a sad, sad commentary on where separation on grounds of conscience can lead. On that unhappy note we leave the Seceders for the moment, though the next chapter will again take up their story.

Thomas Gillespie
At this point we turn to a quite different story, that of the other prominent conscientious objector, Thomas Gillespie, Minister at Carnock — a quiet, amiable, inoffensive man whom one should never have imagined for the part either of leader or of martyr. He had an interesting background. Most of his education he had received at Edinburgh University as a student for the ministry of the Church of Scotland, but before his course was completed he had gone to Perth to study with William Wilson who was preparing men for the Secession ministry. Dissatisfied, apparently, with his experience of the seceders, he stayed only a few days before moving to England and finishing his course at Northampton under Dr Doddridge, an Independent. It was here that he was ordained. Returning north he was inducted to Carnock in 1741. He was a man of no particular brilliance, but was of the faithful, devoted type that must always form the backbone of the parish ministry.

Since the departure of Erskine and his friends in 1733 things had gone from bad to worse in the matter of patronage. Patrons were becoming more inclined to insist on their rights; the crown, which was patron of many parishes, was following a policy of presenting known Moderates to the great annoyance of what was coming to be called the Evangelical party within the Kirk; cases of disputed settlements were increasing in number and becoming more disputatious;

ill-founded complaints were being levelled at presentees whose only fault was that they were not the free choice of the congregation. What was even more disturbing was that in many cases Presbyteries were genuinely at a loss to know how to act, and more and more were becoming unwilling to act at all where local opposition was strong — strong, often, in a physical no less than in a moral sense. It would not be fanciful to discover the original of the modern picket-line in the reception-party which greeted the Presbytery as they arrived to carry through the service of induction of an unwanted presentee.

It was this kind of situation that gave birth to the Riding Committee. Where a presentation had been duly made by the patron but objected to by the parishioners, the Presbytery would refer the matter to the Assembly and they were almost bound to find in favour of the presentee and to instruct the Presbytery to proceed. When the Presbytery resorted to one excuse after another for delay, or when they flatly refused to proceed, the Assembly — which after all consisted of members of Presbyteries who had themselves been in the same tight corner on their home ground — were reluctant to press the point, and the difficulty was got around by appointing a committee of their own number, a Riding Committee, to carry through the induction. The first such appointment was made in 1729 and the next 20 years saw many of them. Whether they were called Riding Committees because they had constantly to be riding hither and yonder or because they had to override the local court I do not know.

The Lanark Case
By the middle of the century things had come to a sorry pass. The case of Lanark shows how confused and difficult — not to say appallingly unjust — the whole system had become. Three patrons each claimed the right to present at Lanark. Since the records showed that the laird had always presented in the past the Presbytery found in his favour and he gave the living to a Mr Dick, a man of great ability and achievement. Unfortunately the laird was most unpopular in the town, so it was not surprising that the Presbytery on arriving to induct was physically assailed by an angry mob and had to depart. Some months later, at the instigation of the Synod,

KIRK CREED AND CHRISTIAN CONSCIENCE 63

Mr Dick was inducted to the church and parish of Lanark in the Tron Kirk in Glasgow — a farcical enough solution in all conscience.

While all this was going forward the crown was pressing its claim to the patronage, a claim upheld successively by the Court of Session and the House of Lords. So, four years after being inducted, Mr Dick was found not to be minister at Lanark at all, he received not a penny of stipend for his four years of ministering there, and he found himself with an enormous bill for litigation. That such a situation could arise was a damning commentary on the whole system.

The Torphichen Case

The Torphichen case is no less illuminating — or disturbing. The patron of this ancient parish in West Lothian was the local laird, and when it fell vacant about this time he put up five names and invited the parishioners to make choice of one of these. This might have seemed a happy way of dealing with his right — no-one could have called it tyrannical. Still the parishioners were not satisfied. They petitioned the Presbytery to add a further name, that of a probationer, Mr Turnbull, but this the Presbytery (rightly one might think) refused to do. When a Mr Walker had been chosen from among the five only about a score of names were appended to the call. The Presbytery was worried and referred the matter to the Synod which sustained the call to Mr Walker. The Presbytery appealed to the Assembly, lost there and was instructed to proceed — which by a majority it declined to do.

Next the case came to the Assembly of 1751. The Moderator of the Presbytery appeared at the bar pleading that excitement was running so high throughout the district that ministers would have lost influence among their own people had they gone to Torphichen to induct. It would be nothing short of tyranny, he added, for members of Presbytery to be compelled to act against conscience. The Assembly was not impressed. Instead, a vote of censure was passed and a Riding Committee appointed. By this device a final confrontation was avoided, but it was clear that a new policy was taking shape, a stronger line was going to be taken against those who on grounds of expediency or popularity or even conscience set at naught the commands of a superior court. The last of the Riding Committees had ridden.

The Inverkeithing Case

From the Presbytery of Linlithgow we cross the Forth to the Presbytery of Dunfermline and to the town of Inverkeithing. In 1751 a Mr Andrew Richardson, minister at Broughton, was presented to the parish by the patron in the best legal fashion. He was in every way an excellent minister and had seemed completely acceptable to the people until it was learned that he was the choice of the patron; when finally he had been inducted he proved not only a fine minister but a highly popular one. But there were those in the parish who were hostile to patronage and therefore hostile to Mr Richardson, and so they prepared a call to a Mr Adam, minister of a dissenting congregation in England. When the Presbytery met to deal with the vacancy it found itself presented with two documents — first a completely regular presentation, and secondly a completely irregular call, and it might have seemed that their choice was a simple one. But the Presbytery did not see it that way. Instead of finding in favour of the presentee they decided on the novel step of sending a committee to Inverkeithing to discover whether Mr Richardson's appointment would meet with popular favour. It is not surprising that as a result of its researches the committee found there were those in the parish who would not approve of the appointment — what is surprising is that they found so little real evidence of hostility. The Presbytery now referred the whole matter to the Commission of Assembly.

Twice the case was before the Commission ere reaching the Assembly itself in 1752. By now it was clear this was to be a test case to determine not the Kirk's attitude to patronage (for that was well enough known) but to the question of how far the individual was bound to carry out the orders of the superior courts. The Assembly agreed without a division that Mr Richardson's induction was to go forward and ordered the Presbytery to meet at Inverkeithing the following Thursday for that purpose. It was known there were in the Presbytery three ministers who were in favour of proceeding, so, in order to force the issue, the Assembly decreed that the quorum was to be increased from the normal three to five.

KIRK CREED AND CHRISTIAN CONSCIENCE

The case in favour of this determined attitude had been put forward by William Robertson of Gladsmuir, who argued that if ministers were to be free to disobey the orders of the supreme court that was the end of a Presbyterianism whose very existence depended upon discipline. From the other side the freedom of the individual conscience was advanced — this was the freedom the Reformation had secured and for which the Covenanters had died, and it was to be treasured at all costs. With the age-old tension between law and liberty, all was set for a fight to a finish.

On the day appointed only four ministers appeared at Inverkeithing, and this not being a quorum nothing could be done. When, the following day, this was reported to the Assembly it was resolved that one of the dissident ministers must suffer deposition, and the lot fell on Thomas Gillespie who, certainly, had been the leader. From this day forward it was to be understood that conscientious conviction would not be accepted as a defence aganst the contumacy of disregarding the order of a superior court.

For a second time the battle had been won by the Kirk, and for the second time it was to be won at the price of a secession.

The Second Secession

The Inverkeithing case may be said to have borne its delayed fruit nine years after Gillespie had paid the price of rebellion and to have done so in the Second Secession and the creation of the Presbytery of Relief.

When sentence had been pronounced Gillespie said, 'I desire to receive this sentence of the General Assembly pronounced against me with real concern and awful impressions of the Divine conduct in it, but I rejoice that to me it is given in behalf of Christ, not only to believe in Him, but also to suffer for His sake'. For a time Gillespie preached in the open air until a meeting-house was built for him in Dunfermline and here he continued to labour until his death in 1774.

It was on 22 October 1761 that an historic meeting was held at Colinsburgh in Fife when three ministers met and constituted the Presbytery of Relief 'for the relief of Christians oppressed in their Christian privileges'. There was

Thomas Gillespie himself; and then there was Thomas Colier, a native of Fife who had been ministering to a dissenting congregation in Westmorland and who had returned north to a meeting-house built in Colinsburgh by a large group of dissatisfied members of the parish of Kilconquhar; and lastly there was Thomas Boston, son of the famous Boston of Ettrick, who in similar circumstances had opened a meeting-house in Jedburgh. The Second Secession from the Kirk was an accomplished fact — 28 years after the First.

Though they may be seen as having sprung from a common cause, the two Churches of the conscientious secessions were vastly different in character and outlook. To some extent this may be traced to differences in their leadership, for it would be hard to conceive two people less alike than Erskine and Gillespie. The former, as we have seen, was self-confident and even spiritually arrogant, while the latter was self-effacing and apologetic. The Secession Church was so sure of itself and so committed to the Covenants as to be bound to break up into sects (as it was already doing in 1761); the Relief Church, on the other hand, had no time for the Covenants, it wanted neither part nor lot with the civil magistrate who it believed had no concern in ecclesiastical affairs, and it showed a spirit of tolerance quite foreign to its time in welcoming to the Lord's table members of all denominations. Its students were trained along with those of the Church of Scotland in the Divinity Faculties. Gillespie himself never wholly lost his affection for the established Kirk and on his deathbed advised his congregation to seek readmission — as, some little time afterwards, they did.

It was not for nearly a century — 1847 to be precise — by which time most of the rents in the ranks of the Seceders had been knit together, that the Secession and the Relief were able to come together to form the United Presbyterian Church.

We have seen, then, how in these two so different cases, under the guidance of two so different men, the battle of conscience was joined with the establishment. The Kirk won as, if she is to be sole judge in her own cause, she is bound to win; but the price of her victory was the loss of a considerable part of her membership and, what in some respects was far more important, a serious diminution in her power and influence in the land; for now any who disliked her rule had other places of Christian meeting to which they could attach themselves. What had been to all intents and purposes the Kirk's monopoly of religion in Scotland was at an end — part of the price she had had to pay if she was to remain sole judge.

References
1 Heron, Alasdair I C, (ed.) (1982). *The Westminster Confession in the Church Today*. The Saint Andrew Press, Edinburgh, p16.
2 Henderson, G D. (1977). *The Church of Scotland: a short history*. The Saint Andrew Press, Edinburgh, Reissued edn, p105.
3 McKerrow, John (1841). *History of the Secession Church*. Glasgow.

IV

Auld Lichts an' a' That

Negative and Exclusive
An apocryphal story tells of a 20th-century Robinson Crusoe who, having spent many years on a desert island, was in process of being rescued by a party from a cruising vessel which by chance had come ashore to take some pictures. Before leaving what for so long had been his home he was showing his rescuers some of the things he had done and made. Finally he took them to a little building topped by what looked like a steeple. 'This,' he said, 'is my Kirk which I erected very early on and which has meant more to me than I can possibly say. Every Sunday morning I have come along here. I have sat quietly, have read a passage of Scripture and said a prayer — sometimes I've even sung a bit of a hymn. You've no idea how much it has helped me.' As they were leaving, the captain of the ship enquired, 'Tell me, that little building over there, that also looks rather like a church'. 'O yes,' said Robinson, 'that is a church — that is the church I don't go to.'

If I may I would add a second story — a true one this time. I began my own ministry as an Assistant in Springburn in a day when that was one of the most densely populated areas in Glasgow. I clearly remember one Sunday morning when every one of the 1200-odd seats which the church provided was filled for Communion — a quite unforgettable sight I found it. The following day I was doing some visiting, as my custom was, and was in the house of one of our most faithful members, a lady who for want of a better term I shall say was of an intensely holy type. Something was said about the service the previous morning and I commented upon how deeply I had been impressed. 'Ah yes,' she said in tones that were much less than enthusiastic, 'quite nice, quite nice. But we've got to remember it's where two or three are gathered together that Christ has promised to be in the midst.' I felt duly chastened.

These two stories seem to illustrate rather well two attitudes to religion which were very common in, and which played a large part in shaping the life of, the Secession fold in the latter half of the 18th century. They might be described respectively as the negative and the exclusive approach.

There are those who derive as much moral satisfaction from contemplating the many, varied, and shameful vices which do not happen to afflict them as they do from the thought of the few virtues with which they chance to be endowed; they draw as much strength from a consideration of the errors, heresies, and false doctrines which mislead their neighbours as from the deep truths they themselves are able to accept; their approach, in a word, is a purely negative approach. These are the folk of the-Church-I-don't-go-to mentality.

From our earliest years we have all known the fallacy involved in converting the proposition that all carrots are vegetables into the affirmation that all vegetables are carrots. But it would seem that not all of us detect any fallacy in equating the statement that if you are a true disciple of Jesus you will be one of a small persecuted company with the declaration that if you are one of a small persecuted company you must be a true follower of Jesus. There are many like my Springburn friend genuinely convinced that because Jesus promised not to neglect the little company of two or three He must have a horror of crowds. You remember James Renwick's description of the remnant of the Covenanters which I quoted in an earlier place as 'a poor, wasted, wounded, afflicted, bleeding, misrepresented and reproached Remnant and Handful of suffering people'. How loud and clear the message rings out that if you are all of these things then you are bound to be right. This is the exclusive approach, the small-is-beautiful position. These are the folk of the two-or-three-gathered-together mentality.

Growth of the Secession
In our last chapter we noted three significant milestones along the early road of the Secession Church — first 1733

when the Associate Presbytery was formed, the ministers involved, however, continuing in their parishes though the pastoral tie had been severed by the Assembly; then 1736 when the Judicial Testimony was published setting forth the strict Covenanting principles of the group; and lastly 1740 when the eight brethren were finally deposed and legally banned from their pulpits and parishes, though it was to be some little time before all of them had gone. During these seven years the movement had been gaining considerable support. It always happens when there is a monopoly that there are dissatisfied customers who the moment the lock is broken will move to the new supplier, and certainly at this time there were not wanting those throughout the country who were ill-pleased with the Kirk in general and with their own minister in particular. In many cases like this people had found solace in grouping themselves together in Praying Societies, and these now looked to the Secession for sermon if not actually for ministry.

To take a single instance — in Glasgow it is recorded that as early as 1738 a petition bearing the names of 83 members of praying societies in and around the city was presented to the Associate Presbytery asking to be taken under inspection. Their prayer was answered and they had sermon for the first time on a weekday in April 1739 when both of the Erskines came through and tents were erected at a spot in the neighbourhood of Queen's Park where the societies had been meeting for some time past. The congregation was drawn from as far afield as Rutherglen, New Kilpatrick, Cadder, Mearns, Neilston, Kilbarchan and Old Monkland. It was in the following October that James Fisher of Kinclaven, son-in-law of Ebenezer Erskine and one of the original four, was translated as minister, and it was not very long before they had built themselves a large meeting-house in Shuttle Street just off High Street. This pattern was being repeated in many parts of the country and the Secession Church was gathering a large following.

George Whitefield

Their fortunes in these early days, however, were not greatly advanced by an unhappy association with George Whitefield,

AULD LICHTS AN' A' THAT

the famous evangelist who was achieving such spectacular results in many parts of England and in the United States. The Seceders invited Whitefield to Scotland but indicated that they would expect him to renounce his prelatic ordination and to sign the Covenants. For them these were the credentials which alone would establish credibility. He replied to the effect that if he came to Scotland it would be as an itinerant preacher free to proclaim the Gospel wherever opportunity afforded. He came north in 1741, stayed with Ralph Erskine, preached in Dunfermline, and later met with the Associate Presbytery who proceeded to put him right in regard to the Solemn League and Covenant, a document in which he had no faintest interest. They parted on terms which were far from cordial — indeed he was to be denounced by them as an emissary of the devil.

It was some time after Whitefield's departure from Scotland, and quite unconnected with his visit, that there occurred that strange evangelical upheaval known as the Cambuslang wark, an astounding manifestation of what today we should call the charismatic — some speaking in tongues, some beating the breast, some bleeding profusely at the nose, some falling in convulsions. Learning of what was afoot, Whitefield hurried north to share in the experience and at the August communion at which he preached it is reckoned that 30 000 people participated. It is not to be wondered at if not everyone was madly enthusiastic about the Cambuslang wark, and certainly Whitefield's participation in it must have been enough to scunner the leaders of the Secession. Whatever the reason, the fact is that Seceders and Cameronians knew no bounds in their condemnation of the whole affair, James Fisher, Adam Gib and Ralph Erskine being particularly bitter. Not content with denouncing it from their pulpits they went so far as to appoint a day of national mourning and fasting 'for the countenance given to Whitefield, a priest of the Church of England, who had sworn the Oath of Supremacy and abjured the Solemn League and Covenant'. The Cameronians contrived to do even better — they published a Declaration, Protest and Testimony of the suffering remnant of the Anti-Popish, Anti-Lutheran, Anti-Prelatic, Anti-Whitefieldian, Anti-Erastian, Anti-Sectarian true Presbyterian Church of Christ in Scotland against Mr George

Whitefield and his encouragers and against the work at Cambuslang. Can one conceive a more vivid exposition of the churches-I-don't-go-to mentality?

It is not wholly surprising, then, that nearly a century was to pass before a Secession cause was begun in Cambuslang — and that in spite of the fact that a disputed settlement in the parish church had led to a three-years' vacancy, the kind of set-up that could usually be counted on mightily to advance the cause of the Seceders. Even when as late as 1836 the Secession banner was raised at Bushyhills the congregation survived for only ten years, the first minister resigning on health grounds and the second asking to be relieved owing to dissensions within the congregation of which he had been unaware when he accepted the call. The cynic could have said that the effects of the Secession condemnation of the Cambuslang wark were deeper and more lasting than the results of the wark itself!

The Burgess Oath

Trouble of a far more serious kind than the Whitefield affair was awaiting the Secession. Following upon the '45 rebellion in which, as was to be expected, a number of Episcopal clergy were implicated, a new clause was introduced into the oath which every burgess was required to take. It was in these terms, 'I protest before God and your lordships that I profess and allow in my heart the true religion presently professed within the realm and authorised by the laws thereof; I shall abide therein and defend the same to my life's end, renouncing the Romish religion called Papistry'. This was to be the subject of the most terrifying wrangle.

It is said of the Englishman that he has a genius for compromise; I should say that the corresponding quality in the Scot is a genius for controversy. Let the Englishman find a formula which you can interpret in your own way and he in his and to which both of you can put your signatures, then neither of you is going so far to forget his obligations as a gentleman as to ask awkward questions about what the other had in mind when he put down his name. The service of recognition of ministries that marks a union in which Anglicans are involved is a case in point. Here in Scotland, on the other hand, we would fall out over a comma, and until it had been replaced with a semi-colon we would not so much as lift the pen. The Burgess Oath provides a fine example of this. According to the Erskines and those who adhered to them the 'true religion' to which they were subscribing clearly meant their own brand since they and they alone were the true Church. It could not be more simple. What harm could there be in swearing allegiance to that. But inevitably there were also those who said, 'Not so. The words "true religion" unmistakably refer to that so-called religion authorised by law, the religion of the establishment, that accursed bondage from which we have just broken free — to swear fealty to that is to be guilty of perfidy. We dare not allow our people to commit so grievous a sin'.

When the Synod met in April 1746 the issue was hotly debated and a resolution approved that the Burgess Oath should not be taken by any member of the denomination and that anyone who had already taken it must appear before his Kirk Session to make confession of his sin. This was, needless to say, a majority decision and a very large minority protested against it. The debate which had begun in the Synod was soon raging in Kirk Sessions and congregations throughout the land. While one must admire the zeal for strict conscientious propriety evinced, one cannot deny that the amount of heat, not to say ill-will, generated was out of all proportion to the importance of the subject. Or so, at least, it appears today. An interesting feature was that the battle was fought at its fiercest in places like Mearns and Kilbarchan, country parishes in no way connected with the burghs so that the interest in the question was purely academic. For my own part, I find it difficult to be convinced by the Burgher argument that the Oath was inoffensive in their circumstances because it was possible to interpret 'the true religion' as meaning their religion — does not one detect a note here of Jesuitical casuistry? On that basis even Bonnie Prince Charlie himself could nearly have put his name to the paper. At the same time one must admire their determination to find a way to maintain the unity of the denomination rather than see it split over an issue which had no relevance whatever to the business of winning Scotland for Christ.

The Breach

When the Synod convened the following April (1747) two days of ferocious debate ended in open rupture, the Anti-Burghers having a majority, but the Burghers under the guidance of the Erskines standing firm in favour of tolerance, and each claiming to be the true Associate Synod. The Burghers won the Battle of the Name, retaining the title of Associate Synod, while the Anti-Burghers adopted the name of General Associate Synod. At the start this group met in the manse of their unquestioned leader, Adam Gib, of whom Small says, 'when matters of dispute arose worthy of his powers he came down on them like a battle-axe, clear, weighty and decisive'. Which perhaps accounted for the fact that they were so ruthlessly logical and thorough. They instituted a libel against their defaulting brethren, citing them to appear at their bar to answer thereto, and when no appearance was made finding them contumacious. One censure followed another until finally the two Erskines and James Fisher were solemnly consigned to Satan in the sentence of the greater excommunication. While this grand exercise in censuring was going forward in the Synod, a desperate drama of bitterness was being enacted at the grassroots level of the congregations. The affair reflected all the agony and pathos inseparable from civil war — brother fighting against brother, father against son. The Erskines were leaders on the Burgher side yet one of Ralph's sons defected to the Anti-Burgher camp.

The terrifying lengths to which they were prepared — if not positively happy — to go is well illustrated in the case of Patrick Matthew, minister of an Anti-Burgher congregation at Midholm in the Parish of Bowden. In November 1749 a paper was submitted to the Anti-Burgher Presbytery signed by six elders and six members on behalf of that congregation saying that they were 'grieved and offended' at their minister because, having Ralph Erskine as a guest at his manse last August, he joined with him in religious exercises although he well knew that Erskine was under the sentence of the greater excommunication. Matthew admitted that he had allowed Erskine to pray at evening worship in his manse, but he personally saw no harm in that since he had dissented against the excommunication of the brethren. He confessed to

AULD LICHTS AN' A' THAT

wrongdoing, however, and, to satisfy local opinion, he read from the pulpit an extract of the Presbytery's judgment. Three months later the Presbytery took up a new complaint from two elders and 18 members at Midholm averring that the minister still had not given them any satisfaction for his offence in having religious fellowship with Ralph Erskine. By now, understandably, Matthew was getting rattled and proved refractory when making his defence. He was thereupon himself deposed and excommunicated. In that unhappy condition, presumably, he could have as much religious fellowship as he liked with Ralph Erskine. To rub salt into the wound John Erskine, Ralph's defecting son, was chosen to lead the devotions at the meeting of Synod which carried through the act of deposition.

Worse was to come. John Erskine died of a violent fever at the age of 29, and when his father visited him on his deathbed he would not allow him to pray with him. The historian adds, 'Indeed for him to have done otherwise would have been for him to fall into the offence for which the minister of Midholm was brought to the Synod's bar'. And he goes on, 'This is merely saying that he was faithful to the dictates of a misguided conscience even in death'. Would it not have been more accurate to say a 'misguiding' rather than a 'misguided' conscience? It is indeed terrifying to contemplate the lengths to which conscience can misguide us.

This rupture of 1747, generally known as the Breach, was to continue for 70 years and was to leave a heritage of bitterness that would last even longer. And all over the precise meaning of an obscure phrase in an oath which mighty few of the contestants had any obligation to swear. It is an awesome lesson about the extremes of persecuting zeal, intolerance and blind hatred that can follow upon that extremity of conviction that we call the guiding of conscience.

So with 'the Breach' we have reached the first fork on the road of the Seceders. In 1733 it had all begun as the Associate Synod, and here we are, 14 years later, with the Associate Synod and the General Associate Synod, with Burghers and Anti-Burghers.

The Lifter Controversy

The feverish excitement of the Breach having subsided, things moved reasonably smoothly in both branches, enlivened, it has to be said, by the occasional deposition or even excommunication of a minister for this offence or for that until 1782 when the Anti-Burgher camp was disturbed by the 'Lifter' controversy. By comparison with the Burgher issue this was a mere flutter in the doo-cot although it did generate a fair amount of heat and led to the formation of a new, if short-lived, Presbytery of Anti-Burgher Non-Lifters.

The moving spirit in this controversy was one David Smyton, minister at Kilmaurs. He had gone there in 1740, long before the Breach, and, thanks to a legacy, a church with sittings for a thousand had been built in the village though his duties took him much further afield, involving in the course of the year six Sundays at each of Fenwick and Dalry and two at Kilwinning. On the occurrence of the Breach, Mr Smyton sided at first with the Burghers, though some months later he appeared before the Anti-Burgher Presbytery of Edinburgh with confession of his sins and compliances.

It would seem that at this time the practice had come to be accepted among many Anti-Burghers of not lifting the bread and wine at the time of their consecration in the service of Communion. In 1782 Smyton sought to make an issue of this, demanding that the practice of non-lifting be stopped. Jesus, he said, took bread before He blessed it, and conformity to His example ought to be enforced. The Synod — surprisingly perhaps in view of its past form — was not prepared to make an issue of this; they refused to insist on any particular practice, leaving the choice to the individual minister. The leader in this plea for tolerance was none other than Adam Gib, who, it is generally believed, had been responsible for the innovation in the first place, but whom one might have thought ill-cast for the role of tolerance-pleader. Still, he carried the day, and after a deal of to-ing and fro-ing the Synod in September enjoined forbearance. Mr Smyton, however, declined the Synod's authority and was suspended from the exercise of his ministry. With most of his congregation he left the Anti-Burgher fold. For him the matter was one of crucial importance, which is to say it was a matter of conscience — for the question was nothing less than 'whether the example of the Great Head of the Church is to be the rule of administration or not'. On any matter where the line of duty is so clearly defined freedom for me to do what is right is of little worth if others are at liberty to do what is wrong.

Although Smyton's cause seems to have been substantially enough defeated at the Synod he was not wholly without support — Kilwinning, Greenock, Paisley and Beith sided with him. The Anti-Burgher congregation in Beith, for example, was utterly rent in two over the matter. Of a similar situation in Glasgow's mother Anti-Burgher congregation it was said that it was 'a tempestuous time in Session and out of it, chiefly because those engaged in it would listen to no instruction, hear no reasoning, bear no contradiction'. The Seceding congregation in the town of Dalry had thrown in their lot with the Burghers, but at this juncture a new Anti-Burgher cause was founded in the town for no other purpose than to serve those from a fairly wide area around who sided with Mr Smyton on the Lifter issue. They called a Mr John Gemmell to be their minister and there they continued for 40 years until Mr Gemmell emigrated to Ontario. Small tells us that an old lady with whom he spoke remembered little about them except that towards the close they had frequent meetings and 'a great deal of quarrelling'.

The other principal figure occupying part of the Lifter stage was Mr Josiah Hunter, minister of the Anti-Burgher congregation in Falkirk. For many years things had not been well between Mr Hunter and a group within his congregation, though he appears to have enjoyed the loyal support of his people generally. Scarce a Synod passed, we read, without some complaint coming up from Falkirk. Over and over again the Synod seemed to have been successful in restoring peace only to discover trouble breaking out afresh. Finally in 1780 the Synod rebuked Mr Hunter, in response to which he told them bluntly that their censure was 'null and void, scandalous, partial and injurious to truth'. He was given till next Synod to calm down, but when he appeared then he was in an even more belligerent mood, and so he was deposed. It was at this point that he espoused the cause of Mr Smyton, and these two, along with a Mr Proudfoot of Leith who for long had been carrying on a feud with Adam Gib on other issues, formed a Presbytery which licensed students, ordained ministers, and finally broke up through internal dissension.

As indicated earlier, the Anti-Burgher Non-Lifter Presbytery had a short, if an active, life.

This particular division within the Anti-Burgher ranks was not in the long term of a serious nature, but it does provide a clear enough illustration of what is bound to happen when a man insists on the right not just to have a conscience of his own but to have all others fitted with a conscience of identical pattern.

New Licht — Burghers

We have seen how one Church of the Secession became two at the Breach of 1747. We are now to see how half a century later these two became four, the Burghers splitting as between Auld and New Licht in 1799 and the Anti-Burghers undergoing a similar experience in 1806. We shall begin with the developments in the Burgher camp since they were the first to resolve the conflict — insofar, that is, as splitting into two can be seen as the resolution of a difference.

It was in 1795 that a Mr John Fraser of Auchtermuchty submitted to the Synod a representation in which he sought a relaxation of the Formula presented to all taking office in the Church, and that in two respects — first as regards the powers of the civil magistrate in matters of religion, and secondly in respect of the obligations of the National Covenant upon posterity. Mr Fraser was, he claimed, unhappy with the second question, which asked candidates whether they did sincerely own and believe the whole doctrine contained in *The Westminster Confession*, acknowledging it to be a confession of their own faith; and also with the fourth question, which required acceptance of the perpetual obligation of the Covenants. He himself had no difficulty in these matters, he said, but he did want to guard against a lack of entire harmony between profession and principle. The matter was referred to a committee. The committee reported in due course, recognising that there were areas where there was 'disputation between good and faithful men' but pleading that forbearance should be exercised towards all ministers 'whatever their sentiments be on that article'.

Meantime an interim position was adopted, amending the two disruptive questions, hedging them about with explanations and reservations so that one could be forgiven for thinking they were at one and the same time holding firmly to the *status quo* and moving relentlessly forward from it. Final judgment was to be delayed till 1797. The intensely interesting thing is that now at last among these men of conscience there was emerging a recognition that there might be 'good and faithful men' who saw things differently and that provision should be made for such. Nor will it have escaped notice that we are now talking about 'sentiments' and not about conscientious convictions.

As must have been anticipated, the idea of change on this scale did not commend itself to the Church as a whole. The Synod when it met in 1797 had before it 41 petitions from Kirk Sessions and congregations, only nine being completely in favour of change and six seeking delay — which left 27 solid against. After long debate Mr Fraser's petition was dismissed and instead of the complicated questions there was substituted a complicated Preamble to the whole Formula giving the same impression of saying Yes and No at the same time and with equal emphasis.

A solution of this kind could scarcely be expected to commend itself universally, so the controversy dragged on till the Synod of 1799 when it was decided they should return to what had been their interim position.

Auld Licht — Burghers

At this point, needless to say, a small number protested and withdrew, proclaiming themselves the true heirs of the Secession. Their protest was in these terms, 'I protest ... that as the Synod has obstinately refused to remove the Preamble prefixed to the Formula, and declare their simple and unqualified adherence to our principles, I will no more acknowledge them as over me in the Lord until they return to their principles'. This body came to be known as the Original Burgher Synod, or the Auld Licht Burghers.

It is most enlightening to recognise that the question ultimately at issue in this separation was not a question about the binding force upon the individual of either the Confession or the Covenants, but a question about the right of the Church itself to change its position in relation to these. The point was well brought out in course of some pamphleteering that went on after the division had occurred. Mr

Proudfoot, a minister of the Church of Scotland, had poured scorn on the idea of a standard 'that may be varied at pleasure'. From the New Licht side a Mr Peden agreed that 'it is nonsense if by "at pleasure" you mean the personal pleasure of every private individual of a society; but if you mean by it the pleasure of the society of which he is a member it is sound sense. The private individual is not at liberty to employ lighter weights or smaller measures than the standard, nor to believe differently from the standard book. But the authority which appointed the standard has the right to alter it'. Interesting, is it not, how we are drifting away from the liberty of the individual conscience towards the doctrine that the Church itself shall be sole judge.

New Licht — Anti-Burgher

To take up now the parallel story of how new light dawned upon the Anti-Burghers. Although it took longer to bring the debate to a conclusion the issue had been raised at an earlier date — 1791 in fact. The problem of the relation of Church and State had been a much chewed-over bone of contention. Calvin had declared that civil government was designed to cherish and support the external works of God, to preserve the pure doctrine of religion, and to defend the constitution of the Church. The Church of Scotland, while she might not have been prepared to go so far as that, had always defended the principle that Church and State could not exist apart, that each owed duties to, and was entitled to expect support from, the other. Away back in the 1720s a totally different conception had been advocated by John Glas of Tealing who, from a vigorous assault on the Covenants, had moved to an attack on the civil establishments of religion, maintaining that the Church was a purely spiritual society which had nothing whatever to do with the State. Glas was deposed in 1729, but this, strictly, was for contumacy and not for his Voluntary philosophy. He founded a sect known in Scotland as Glassites and in England as Sandemanians (after his son-in-law) but it attracted little support.

An interesting side-light was thrown on the subject of the relation of Church and State in Anti-Burgher thinking when in 1759 the Synod considered a proposal to lay before the King its 'grievances concerning the present state of religion in these lands, together with a dutiful and suitable redress for the same'. This was strenuously resisted by that man of so many strenuous resistances, Adam Gib, on the plea that this was going far beyond the Scripture requirement for obedience to the civil power in all matters lawful. He carried his objection. Two years later a similar fate overtook a suggestion for sending a loyal address to King George III on his accession, this time the ground being that since the law did not recognise them as a Church court the proposed address could not constitutionally be received. Carrying consistency a bit far, one might have thought. What Gib was doing was not directing the Synod away from a constitutional cul-de-sac but directing it into a road clearly sign-posted for Voluntaryism.

The New Licht issue arose for the Anti-Burghers in this wise. In 1791 two of their probationers took the unusual step of indicating that they were not prepared to go forward to ordination unless in putting the second of the prescribed questions the Moderator indicated their reservations in regard to it. This, you remember, was the question which required that the candidate 'sincerely owns and declares the whole doctrine contained in the Confession of Faith' as his personal confession. The Presbytery of Glasgow referred the matter to the Synod which in 1796 passed a Declaratory Act that recalled the original reservations regarding the civil power contained in the 1647 Act and substituted others whose effect was to make still wider the gulf between Church and State, and went on to say that while not implying 'the smallest reflection on the venerable compilers of the Confession' the degree of light enjoyed by them seemed to have led them to invest civil rulers with a degree of power inconsistent with 'the spirituality, freedom and independence of the Kingdom of Christ'.

All this time work was proceeding on the revision of the Testimony of the Anti-Burghers, resulting in 1799 in a new 'Acknowledgment of Sins and Engagement to Duties'. As was to be expected, objection was taken to the whole proceeding and in particular to 'those late innovating Acts'. Ironically enough one of the leading objectors was none other than Thomas McCrie, one of the two probationers whose scruples had set the whole affair in motion. Work went on in face of the protest, however, and in 1804 the revised Testimony was submitted to the Synod. This explained that the Westminster Confession was 'not at all the rule of what we are bound to believe, but a public declaration of what we do believe'; it went on to claim the right 'in view of any further light which may afterwards arise from the Word of God, to change its mind on any article of divine truth'; it laid the foundation of a new Voluntaryism in the declaration that the Church is a spiritual kingdom but the State is a secular kingdom and neither kingdom has power over the other; and it acknowledged 'the continuing obligation of the Covenants upon persons of all ranks and their posterity'. In passing it may be appropriate to comment on the distinction drawn between the Westminster Confession as a statement of what we must believe and a statement of what in fact the Church does believe. If in order to stay in the Church we have to accept the whole doctrine of the Confession (the alternative being expulsion) then the Confession is bound to represent a statement of where we do stand and the Testimony has discovered a distinction where there is no difference.

Auld Licht — Anti-Burghers

When in 1806 the revised Testimony was finally adopted by the Anti-Burghers a group of six ministers protested and separated under the leadership of Archibald Bruce of Whitburn. For him this subject must have represented familiar ground, for nearly 20 years earlier he had earned the considerable ill-will of the redoubtable Adam Gib who accused him of advancing principles 'meant to subject the conscience of Christians to the lordship of civil powers, and transferring to these powers the spiritual privileges and business of the Church'. At Whitburn the six established the headquarters of the new body — though they, of course, would not have agreed it was a new body, it was the one true and genuine continuance of the old body. They called it the Constitutional Associate Presbytery, though they will always be better known and more easily identified as the Auld Licht Anti-Burghers, and, if you want to be very comprehensive — and negative — you can add, 'Non-Lifters'. If you want to show just how negative they were you can say that the principal plank in their platform was Anti-Voluntaryism. Another fine example, surely, of the church-I-don't-go-to principle.

It could well be argued that the Secession of 1733 had been born out of intense religious conservatism, and in this sense the Auld Licht Anti-Burghers could claim to be its true progeny, a body which in a day of intellectual ferment was seeking to be more true to the standards of the past than the past itself had ever been. Indeed it would not be difficult to trace the genealogy of the group straight to the Covenanters.

We may now be said to have seen how the one Secession Church of 1733 had by 1806 become four (and even at that with simplifying things by leaving out the Non-Lifters) — there was the Original Burgher Synod (the Auld Licht Burghers), the Associate Synod (the New Licht Burghers), the Constitutional Associate Presbytery (the Auld Licht Anti-Burghers), and the General Associate Synod (the New Licht Anti-Burghers). If the Constitutional Associate Presbytery might be regarded as the true lineal descendant of the Secession, it would be no less true to add that the fragmentation and schism of these 70 years was the inescapable outcome of that same Secession of 1733.

Reunion

As we have reached the end of the 18th century so mercifully we have reached the end of the breakaway story and we move into a new century, one which in the providence of God was to see the healing of most of the breaches, of which there had been so many. The first of these unions was achieved by the coming together of the two New Licht denominations. Both of them were by this time thirled to the Voluntary attitude and this helped; besides, by now the Burgess Oath had been repealed, so there was nothing to keep them apart — though, as we know, old sores are ill to heal and people who had parted for one reason often stay apart for a quite different reason — or for none at all. In 1820, then, the New Licht Burghers and the New Licht Anti-Burghers became the United Secession Church.

There is a well-known principle in ecclesiastical affairs neatly illustrated in the joke about the village where there used to be two Churches, but then they had a union and now there are three. Inevitably there were those who could not see their way to let bygones be bygones — this time from the Anti-Burgher side as it happened — and they stayed out of the union, pursuing their own lonely way as the Protesters for seven years until they united with the Constitutional Associate Presbytery (the Auld Licht Anti-Burghers whom we recently left at Whitburn) to form the Original Seceders.

In 1839 the Original Burgher Synod (the Auld Licht Burghers) found their way back into the main stream of the Church of Scotland, a step made easier for both sides because this group had never wavered in their conviction that a close link should be maintained between Church and State. It might be added that for most of those affected their stay in the Auld Kirk was to be a brief one — four years later they had left in the Disruption.

In the case of this union too the principle that one and one unite to make three applied and a group hived off, the Remanent Auld Licht Burghers. In 1842 this group found it possible to throw in its lot with the Original Seceders (that is, you remember, Constitutionals plus Protesters) to form the Remanent Original Secession Church; but again the one plus one equals three rule proved good and a small party from the Anti-Burgher side went off on its own.

During the 80 years or so while all this was happening the Relief Church had been going steadily on bearing its witness and, relatively speaking, gaining considerable strength. It had been completely unaffected by the spirit of schism, not a single division having broken its ranks. One cannot but wonder whether this is to any extent to be attributed to the fact that from the very outset the Relief had eschewed all allegiance to the Covenants. It will be remembered that they had early espoused the attitude to Church–State relations that was by this time coming to be referred to as the Voluntary principle and that had been adopted by the two branches of the Secession that had seen the new light and that now formed the United Secession Church where the principle was strongly held. The path towards the coming together of these two bodies was now clear — though many Seceders still had grave reservations about open communion — and in 1847 they united to form the United Presbyterian Church — the UPs as they were to be known for the next half-century.

It could be said, then, that by the middle of the 19th

century conscientious objections had for all practical purposes been gathered into one fellowship, the United Presbyterian Church — the significant exception being, of course, the Remanent Auld Licht body. But then by the middle of the 19th century the Disruption had occurred and the Kirk in Scotland was split as it never had been split before. But that is another story and one for the next chapter.

Congregational Fraction

Once a Church has itself set an example of division on matters of comparatively slender moment congregations will be very quick to follow in the wake. The story of Secession congregations abounds in examples of this. I take three interesting cases from my own Presbytery of Glasgow.

The mother Anti-Burgher congregation in Glasgow consisted of those who had marched out of Shuttle Street at the time of the Breach. They had gone to premises in the Cow Loan (now Queen Street), then to Havannah Street, then through the wall to Duke Street where in 1801 they erected a most ambitious building derisively referred to by their unfriends as the Anti-Burgher Folly. In April 1835 their fourth minister, Walter Duncan, was deposed on account of some indiscretion, not, it should be said, of a doctrinal nature. Part of the congregation proceeded very properly towards filling the vacancy, but there was a substantial group in the congregation who were confident that the young man would be restored and who therefore wanted the seat kept warm for his return. The former party were, naturally, upheld by the Presbytery. The others walked out. They acquired a site close by in Regent Place and erected a 1300-seater church, without, let it be added, having paid for it. Shortly thereafter they appealed to the Synod to have Mr Duncan restored so they could present him with a call, but, unhappily for them, the crave of their petititon was refused. Worse was to follow, for Mr Duncan now cut adrift from the Synod and set up his independent standard, conducting services in the Trades Hall, whither most of his fervent admirers followed him. And so the new cause found itself without a congregation, without a minister, without any funds, and without any future, but with a fine new 1300-seater church and with a fine big bill to pay for it. That in brief compass is the story of the ten years that marked the whole life-span of the congregation of East Regent Place.

Another example taken from 20 years earlier in the story of the same mother Anti-Burgher congregation, then in Duke Street. In 1817 a petition was presented to the Kirk Session from a group of members asking to have the reading of the line in the praise of the sanctuary restored and to have the use of repeating tunes discontinued. The Session refused to interfere saying this was the minister's province. The group now approached the Presytery asking to be formed into a separate congregation, and after investigating the extent of their support the Presbytery agreed to this, and the congregation of Regent Place was established, and a building erected almost cheek-by-jowl with that from which they had come — within earshot, I should have thought, of the repeating tunes. It is interesting that when they called their first minister a competing call came from Nicholson Street in Edinburgh. In the Synod, we are told, it required eight hours' discussion before it was resolved he should go to Glasgow. One is entitled to think there must have been some repeating arguments — if not repeating tunes — to take all that long.

I take a last example and, 'to keep the balance fair in ilka quarter', I take it from the Burgher side — it is a story both of a division and of a walk-out. Trouble had arisen in the Burgher congregation in Pollokshaws over the calling of a minister and the case had gone to the superior courts which had decided in favour of a Mr Moscrip. The disaffected party was fairly large and included the elders, so they walked out and formed a congregation of their own. Mr Moscrip died within ten years of his induction and in course of the vacancy the congregation decided to leave the Secession fold and go over to the Free Kirk, the reason being that the Secession Presbytery had criticised the way in which their minutes were being kept. It could hardly be called a conscientious objection.

So we end as we began with fraction on the slightest provocation, and that both within the Church itself and within its constituent congregations. This, it would seem, is the end of the road that begins in conscientious objection, the *reductio ad absurdum* of the doctrine that each man is the measure of truth.

I have often thought that an Auld Licht Anti-Burgher Non-Lifter must have been an intensely interesting ecclesiastical specimen, worthy, surely, of a place in the Burrell Collection. It is all an awesome warning of where slavish obedience to the leading of conscience can bring you.

Conclusion
Having begun this chapter with a story, I may be allowed to end it with another. It comes from the time when men's shirts with collars attached were first making their appearance, the standard pattern up to that time having ended in a neck-band to which a collar was attached with the aid of a couple of studs. A Scotsman went into a London store and asked for a shirt. A selection of the new model was laid out on the counter. He examined them carefully. 'No, no,' he said, 'I'm not wanting a pyjama jacket, I want a shirt, I want a proper shirt, I want a shirt the way God meant a shirt to be.'

We have seen some of the ramifications of the doctrine that a man is entitled to belong to a Kirk organised the way God meant a Kirk to be, and how if you carry out that principle far enough you end up with every man having his own Kirk.

But before we laugh too heartily let us see what lies at the end of the other road, for the doctrine that the Church itself shall be sole judge also has its *reductio ad absurdum*. The conviction that great mother-Church knows best, she will decide what is true, and all that is required of you is to accept that and believe it, that was the doctrine which created the Inquisition, which lit the fires of Smithfield, which filled the air of Scotland with the reek of Patrick Hamilton's burning. That was where we started and we have come round full circle. It is a thought worth pondering.

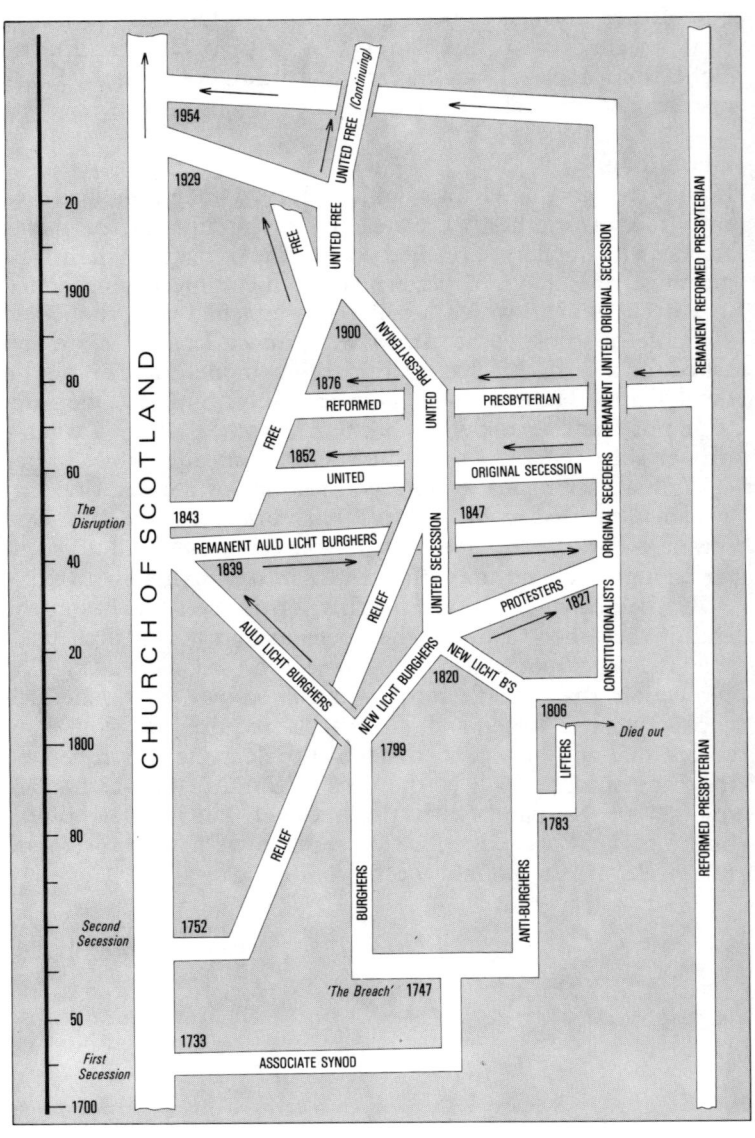

V

Courts of the Kirk and Courts of the Kingdom

Patronage

From the time when it was re-enacted in 1712 until it was repealed in 1874, the Law of Patronage hung like a great black cloud over the Kirk, and to its baneful influence can be traced, at second if not at first hand, most of the ills that afflicted her during that century and a half.

The system which produced patronage was in essence a good one. From the time of the Reformation the services of religion were in every parish in Scotland available absolutely free to all the people of the parish. This was possible because the heritors provided out of the fruits of the earth a stipend for the minister; they also erected and maintained a church capable of seating two-thirds of all the people of the parish over the age of 12; and they provided a manse with suitable 'offices', garden and glebe. Since they were doing all these things it was not unnatural — nor, some might have thought, unreasonable — that they should choose the minister who was to enjoy all the benefits they were thus providing. Once nominated by the patron the presentee had to satisfy the Presbytery as to his moral character and his academic qualifications. The Presbytery then inducted him in a service which at once bound him faithfully to discharge the duties of minister of the parish and made him, as it were, infeft in all its temporal benefits. At the point of presentation the rights of the patron came to an end — he could not in any way direct or control the minister in the exercise of his ministry, nor could he at his own hand do anything to terminate that ministry.

As we saw above, the system of patronage was scrapped in the Revolution Settlement of 1690, and for the next 22 years a rough and ready arrangement was resorted to whereby all the heritors of the parish along with the elders were given the duty and invested with the power to put forward a name. This was not introducing a new system; it was just a half-hearted compromise which continued the basic idea of patronage but put the power of presenting into different hands. The fact that it did not work particularly well made it all the easier under Jacobite pressure to get the old position restored in 1712.

It was not long ere troubles began — as they were bound to do. The whole conception ran contrary to the spirit of the age. A developing sense of democracy resented the idea of the laird dictating to the parishioners in a matter so intensely personal as the choice of their minister. They were under his thumb in too many other directions already — when it came to the cure of their souls they had a right to be independent. As we have seen, it was as early as 1733 that things got to the stage where patronage triggered off the events that led to the Secession of that year. Presbyteries came to have a great deal of sympathy for congregations which had a minister imposed upon them and were quick to play the game of non-co-operation, to find excuses for not taking their part in the business of inducting unwelcome incumbents. Hence the Riding Committee which saw the law fulfilled while avoiding a showdown at local Presbytery level. We saw too the situation that developed at Torphichen, and at Inverkeithing, and how a growing determination on the part of the Assembly to ensure that the law was obeyed whether the people approved of its results or not led to yet another secession and to the appearance in 1761 of the Presbytery of Relief.

For some years thereafter things continued on their unhappy course. Within the Assembly there was an intense dislike of patronage and a desire to see the law changed, but on the other hand there was recognition that, standing the law, the duty of the Church courts was clear and inescapable — to take the presentee on trials, and if these were sustained to go on and induct him. Congregations continued to resist, often to the point of rioting; disputed settlements leading to vacancies protracted over many years came to be the order of the day; vast numbers of decent faithful folk were driven out of the Establishment into the ranks of the Seceders through sheer impatience with the whole miserable business.

Church Extension

In the early 1800s, a new factor emerged. The need for more churches consequent on the great population upsurge of the Industrial Revolution had a marked influence on the patronage question. Small towns had become vast, villages had grown out of recognition, and new communities had sprung up in out-of-the-way corners far distant from the parish church. Something had to be done to provide for the spiritual needs of these people; the old parish system designed for an agricultural economy was fast becoming obsolete. The first step to be taken was the creation of collegiate charges in some of the larger towns — that is to say, two ministers were appointed to function within the one building as ministers of a First and a Second Charge. Each of the men had a full charge, with stipend paid out of teind and a manse provided by the heritors, and each had been presented by a patron. Some intensely interesting human situations were created by these odd juxtapositions, but the provision did little or nothing to meet the growing need. So a further step was taken, legislation being introduced whereby the burghs were to provide churches, stipends, and manses, and in these cases the magistrates enjoyed the right of presentation. In passing it is interesting to note that there seems to have been a certain lack of imagination on the part of the bailies when it came to choosing names — High, Low, and Middle seem as far as they generally got.

The demand for more religious ordinances continued to keep ahead of the supply, so the Chapel of Ease made its appearance, and the number of these steadily increased. When a local community was able and willing to maintain a cause, erect a church, and pay a stipend, this could be erected into a Chapel. After all, congregations in the Secession tradition had been doing just this for many a long year, so why need the Establishment lag behind? The result, however, was the creation of a kind of two-tier ministry, the ministers of the chapels of ease having no Kirk Session, no parish, and no seat in Presbytery.

With so complete a revolution occurring in the whole character of ministry and with so many additions to the ranks of the ministry, ideas were changing radically on the whole question of patronage and there was steadily building up a majority of people prepared to contest the issue, and indeed ready — in some cases even happy — to defy the law should the need arise. The whole thing began to take a very definite shape in 1834 with the passing by the Assembly of two most important and significant pieces of legislation, the Veto Act and the Chapels Act. It was the insistence of the Kirk that she was going to operate these two Acts let the law of the land be what it might which led to the confrontation between the courts of the Kirk and the courts of the Kingdom, from which arose the Kirk's claim to be sole judge in all matters in which her interests were affected. It was when she was defeated in that struggle that there followed the great upheaval known as the Disruption. It is essential, therefore, that we look rather closely at these Acts that were to be the cause of results so extraordinary and far-reaching.

The Veto Act
From very ancient times the induction of a minister to a parish, while it began with a presentation by the patron, required also a call by the congregation. The call had nothing whatever to do with choosing the person to be inducted — that choice had already been made — but was, as it were, an expression of concurrence by the members and a promise to the new minister of their loyalty and support. This quality of the call as no more than a promise of support to a new minister was well brought out in days long after patronage had gone and congregations used to hear and vote upon a long leet of candidates. Let it be that I had put my cross opposite the name of Mr A. After the votes had been counted it was Mr D who was declared elected. I found no difficulty in signing the call to the said Mr D — he would not have been my choice but he was the choice of the majority and he could count on me as a loyal supporter. It is in the same spirit that today's Church Extension congregation subscribes a call to a minister chosen for them by an Assembly Committee. I say all this to show that there is a distinct difference between having liberty of choice and signing a call.

New ideas were abroad at this time and men were asking whether acceptability to the congregation was not every whit as relevant as a knowledge of Hebrew and Greek; they were saying that what the Presbytery had to judge was the man's ability to discharge a fruitful ministry in this particular parish and that in such a situation his ability to win the promise of the loyal support of the members should be a deciding factor. So the call was coming to be seen as a piece of vital evidence when the presentee was on his trials, for if only a handful of members have promised a minister their support, encouragement and prayers, is there any hope of his ministry amongst them being successful? If they create a riot to prevent his induction, what possibility is there of his ministry being richly blessed?

At the Assembly of 1832 no fewer than 11 overtures were tabled, all of them asking the Assembly to take steps to have the call restored to what was called its 'constitutional efficiency'. Instead the Assembly found that any attempt to make a well-signed call a *sine qua non* of induction lay beyond the competence of the Kirk so long as patronage continued on the statute-book. The issue was raised again the following year, following upon 65 overtures being presented. A motion was advanced that a committee be appointed to consider how a presentation could be frustrated should a majority of the people dissent, with or without reason, and it was on an extremely tight vote that this was defeated. It was becoming ominously obvious how things were moving.

The next year (1834), the Veto Act was duly passed, ordaining that 'it shall be an instruction to Presbyteries that if, at the moderating of a call to a vacant pastoral charge, the major part of the male heads of families, members of the vacant congregation and in full communion with the Church, shall disapprove of the person in whose favour the call is proposed, such disapproval shall be sufficient ground for the Presbytery rejecting such person'. That is to say, Presbyteries were enjoined to reject any presentee to whom more than half of the heads of families took exception — they were not to judge the value of the objections, merely to count the heads of the objectors. This certainly has all the appearance of being a new condition imported into the operation of patronage and as such an infringement of the law. But before we condemn the Assembly remember that the motion was proposed by Lord Moncrieff, a distinguished Senator of the College of Justice. In following his lead the Assembly could hardly be accused of a reckless disregard of the law!

His Lordship began by showing from a study of Kirk history that it is 'a fundamental law of this Church that no person shall be intruded on any congregation contrary to the will of the people'. He went on to show how at the Revolution Settlement it was given to the elders and heritors to nominate in a vacancy, but it was for the Presbytery to determine whether, having a regard to all the circumstances, the nominee was a suitable person; and he further contended that while the 1712 Act had given back to the patron the right of choosing it had 'altered nothing as to the manner in which the individual is to be presented to the congregation, and it is still in force on this point'. For the other side it was represented that the motion amounted to 'a transfer of the essential right of the Church to judge on all qualifications and the giving to the congregation a co-ordinate voice and authority in this matter, which is at variance with the whole system'. As Dr Mearns expressed it, 'The proposal wrests from Presbyteries all control of judgment in the matter — it renders them purely ministerial: and when a majority of the people, without assigning the slightest cause for it, disapprove the presentee, let the sentiments of the Presbytery in respect of him be what they may ... they must reject the presentation and prevent his admission'. Lord Moncrieff's motion was carried by 184 votes to 139, was converted into an interim Act, was sent down to Presbyteries under Barrier Act procedure, and in 1835 was converted into a standing law of the Church. For better or for worse the Veto Act had arrived.

The Chapels Act
Before they took up the controversial matter of the Veto Act, the Assembly of 1834 had passed what must have seemed to many the quite innocuous Chapels Act. As we have seen, the urgent need for more and yet more churches following upon the great population movement had led to the creation, especially in the more densely populated areas, of Chapels of Ease, which did not have Kirk Sessions of their own, being under the Kirk Session of the parish in which they were situated, and whose ministers did not have seats in Presbytery. The new Act altered all that — it gave the Chapels the same standing *quoad sacra* as the old parishes enjoyed *quoad*

omnia, they were to have Kirk Sessions of their own, parishes were to be carved out for them, and their ministers were to sit in the Church courts. In the Assembly debate the opposition claimed that the creation of new parishes was governed by law, and if the law was inadequate or out of date the only proper course was to enter into consultation with the State with a view to having it altered. Until this was done the chapels should continue with their present status. The so-called Popular Party was very much in the driving-seat at this Assembly and the Chapels Act was approved by 152 votes to 103, was converted into an interim Act, and the following year into a standing law.

Here then in the Assembly of 1834 we find the Kirk asserting its authority — and declaring its autonomy — in a very big way. Whatever may be said in defence of the legality of the Veto Act, it clearly trespassed beyond purely spiritual considerations into a realm where the patrimonial interests of patrons and presentees were affected, for it introduced a new condition into the operation of the civil right of presentation. No less clearly the Chapels Act proclaimed the belief of the Kirk that she had the right to say precisely how new parishes might be erected without any kind of reference to the State. To men of any discernment it was clear that the Kirk was set on a collison course, and it must have been of little comfort to them to realise that so many of their brethren seemed happy that it should be so.

The Auchterarder Case

In the event they had not many miles to travel before the first collision occurred, Auchterarder being the scene of the crash. The facts, briefly, were these. In October 1834 the Parish of Auchterarder being vacant, the local laird, the Earl of Kinnoull, laid before the Presbytery a presentation in favour of Mr Robert Young, a person of admirable character, fully qualified for the post, but a poor preacher. Here was the first opportunity under the new law for the parishioners legally to present their objections, and this they did with no little enthusiasm — only three people signed the call, and 287 heads of families out of 330 in the parish appeared for the purpose of exercising their veto. When the matter came before the Presbytery some appeals were taken on procedural points and the whole matter went to the 1835 Assembly which ordered the Presbytery to proceed in terms of the new Act. This the Presbytery did and on 7 July rejected Mr Young.

This led to an action being raised in the Court of Session at the instance of the patron and the presentee asking that court to find that the Presbytery was bound and astricted to make trial of the qualifications of the presentee and if they found him qualified to admit him as minister of Auchterarder; and to find further that the rejection of the presentee without having taken him on trial, and solely on the veto of the parishioners, was injurious to the patrimonial rights of the presentee and contrary to statute law. The Kirk's claim to be sole judge was to be put to the test. The significance of the case was so clearly recognised that the entire bench of 13 Lords of Session sat for three solid weeks listening to pleadings in which the whole history of the Kirk was rehearsed. After a couple of months' avizandum their Lordships by a majority of eight to five came down in favour of Mr Young. The fact that five learned judges upheld the Kirk's claim is a fact not to be forgotten.

It was now the spring of 1838 and when the Assembly met a few weeks later a sharp spirit of rebellion could be detected. The general impression seemed to be that the Kirk had a perfect right to pass the Veto Act, or any other Act which had reference to spiritual matters, and that any pronouncement by the civil authority upon the legality of such Acts was sheer unauthorised interference not to be tolerated by a Kirk whose constitution was by Divine Right. It was put on record that 'in all matters touching the doctrine, government or discipline of this Church her judicatories possess an exclusive jurisdiction founded on the Word of God', and it was resolved that they would assert and defend this jurisdiction and the supremacy and sole headship of the Lord Jesus Christ, and would firmly enforce submission to this upon their office-bearers and members by the execution of her laws. It would be hard to imagine a more emphatic statement of the doctrine of sole judge — or a more menacing definition of the 'or else' aspect of affairs. The sting, it was said at the time, was in the tail.

Appeal to the House of Lords

Having adopted this Declaration of Independence the Assembly went on to take what appears a strange step — they resolved to appeal the case to the House of Lords. Now if you accept the principle that the civil courts have a jurisdiction then nothing could be more natural or proper than to pursue your case to the highest of these courts and get the business settled once and for all. But if your contention is that the civil courts have no business here then why go to them? It was different in the Court of Session where the initiative had lain with the patron, for there the Kirk was taken to a court whose jurisdiction she repudiated. But here she is of her own volition taking her business to these very courts. The following May, the House of Lords found in favour of the defenders, declared the Veto Act to be illegal, found that the Presbytery was bound to make trial of the presentee's qualifications, and that 'qualifications' was a technical term referring exclusively to life, literature, and doctrine. That was that. What would have happened had the judgment gone the other way — would the Assembly have hailed it as a victory proving the Veto Act to be good law, or would they have seen their Lordships' findings as no more than an interesting irrelevance? In view of the actual verdict the question is itself an interesting irrelevance.

Scarcely had the judgment been given when the Assembly of 1839 met. It was moved that the Veto Act having been found to be illegal Presbyteries be instructed to proceed with the settlement of ministers as in the past. This, however, was very heavily defeated by a motion proposed by Dr Thomas Chalmers in these terms:

> That the Presbytery of Auchterarder be instructed to offer no further resistance to the claims of Mr Young or of the patron to the emoluments of the benefice of Auchterarder; ... and that the Assembly further resolve that the principle of non-intrusion cannot be abandoned, and that no presentee shall be forced upon any parish contrary to the will of the congregation.

The motion went on to seek the appointment of a committee to explore the whole field.

Clearly on the face of it Dr Chalmers' motion is fraught with inconsistencies. For one thing, Mr Young had been presented as minister at Auchterarder, he had not merely been awarded the stipend and other financial benefits of the living. For another thing, it was not enough for the Presbytery to take the negative step of offering no resistance, they had to take the positive steps of judging and inducting. Or again, how can obedience to the law be reconciled with the determination that no unwelcome presentee is ever to be inducted. However subtly the motion might be disguised, it amounted in effect to a declaration by the Kirk that in the matter of the settlement of a minister in a parish she herself would be sole judge — and sole law-maker into the bargain.

Inevitably the matter had to be taken further, and there was a second Auchterarder Case which went to the House of Lords and whose decision probably as much as any single incident precipitated the Disruption. But perhaps we could leave it at that for the moment while we trace the course of another and still more distressing case — that of Marnoch and the Presbytery of Strathbogie. It was in this case that the 'or else' provisions were put into effect.

The Marnoch Debacle

The Parish of Marnoch in the Presbytery of Strathbogie having fallen vacant, a presentation was duly made in favour of a Mr Edwards, a man of considerable ability but apparently deemed a poor preacher, and in any case as the laird's choice certain to be unacceptable. This was abundantly proved when only the local publican and three non-resident heritors signed the call and 261 out of 300 heads of families exercised the veto. The Presbytery sought the guidance of the Synod which in turn passed it up to the Assembly, a body which in the mood then prevailing had no hesitation in saying, 'Reject'. This the Presbytery did. The patron apparently accepted that as final and went on to make a fresh presentation. Before, however, the Presbytery could take any steps in relation to this second choice Mr Edwards went to the Court of Session asking that the Presbytery be declared bound to take him on trials.

This put the Presbytery on the spot. By a majority they resolved:

> that the Court of Session having authority in matters relating to the induction of ministers and having interdicted all pro-

ceedings on the part of the Presbytery; and it being the duty of the Presbytery to submit to their authority, regularly interponed, the Presbytery do delay all procedure until the matter in dispute be finally determined.

To many this might have appeared a prudent decision worthy of shrewd hard-headed Aberdonians; but you will note that it sprang from the premise that the Court of Session has authority in matters relating to the induction of ministers, and that was enough to damn it in the view of others. And these others having a majority in the Commission of Assembly, the Presbytery was censured for its assertion that the Court of Session had any such authority and was prohibited from taking any further steps before the whole Assembly would meet.

Scarcely had the Commission imposed this censure and injunction than the Court of Session decreed that the Presbytery was bound to take Mr Edwards on trial. By this time too the House of Lords had declared the Veto Act illegal. The Presbytery of Strathbogie apparently now felt that its position was clear. It met, sustained Mr Edwards' presentation, appointed his trials, and reported its proceedings to the Commission of Assembly. That body met specifically to deal with the case — and to deal with the Presbytery. The seven ministers were represented by counsel who reported that they adhered to their position. The Commission resolved to annul the whole proceedings of the Presbytery of Strathbogie, to suspend the offending seven from their functions as ministers, to instruct the other four ministerial members of the Presbytery to intimate the sentences in the parishes affected and to be responsible for the ongoing work there. They even appointed an influential committee of Assembly to assist them in what some would regard as their intruding. A totally new position had now emerged. For a minister to recognise the authority of the civil courts in a matter where Church interests were affected had become an ecclesiastical offence carrying the most condign punishment.

Four days after sentence of suspension had been passed upon them, the offenders met as the Presbytery of Strathbogie and applied to the Court of Session for interdict against the others coming in to officiate in their parishes — which, of course, was granted. That, however, did not prevent those appointed by the Commission from going about their business. They respected the power, if they did not acknowledge the authority, of the civil arm to the extent of keeping away from church, church-yard, and schoolhouse, these being the areas designed in the interdict, but they held meetings at church-gates, market squares, and other such-like places, and not unnaturally a keen controversy was aroused. Once more the seven had recourse to the Court of Session against ministers of the Kirk performing ministerial functions in their parishes without their consent. This too was granted and came to be known as 'the extended interdict'. Said the intruders, 'Things are come to a sorry pass when the courts of the land tell us when and where we may preach the Gospel', and they persisted in their ways, but, mercifully, the seven did not press the issue.

The end was not yet even in sight. Mr Edwards who by now had been found qualified for, but not admitted to, Marnoch raised an action in the Court of Session requiring the Presbytery to admit him or pay him £10 000 damages. The Court left the latter option very much alone, but they found that the Presbytery was bound to induct, and they decreed accordingly. Now indeed the Presbytery was faced with a dilemma — probable imprisonment on the one side, almost certain deposition on the other. They chose the latter option. A painful scene ensued. On a bleak January day five ministers appeared to induct Mr Edwards. The church was filled with parishioners whose agent protested against the settlement, saying that he would have given in objections to life and doctrine only that he did not recognise the ministers present as the Presbytery of Strathbogie. In no little confusion and disorder the protesters left the church and the induction was carried through in circumstances which no one could have described as edifying.

Professor Cunningham in his History describes the event thus, 'Five suspended ministers, in defiance of the injunction of their ecclesiastical superiors, and in face of the protestations of the whole people, ordaining a suspended licentiate, and the parishioners to a man deserting the church and riot and uproar ensuing'. An eye-witness of the event is recorded as saying, 'We have seen a young man ordained and welcomed by a religious people with sincere and earnest prayers for his success, but until Thursday last we never saw a minister ordained who had no single parishioner, no human being of his charge, to wish him god-speed and pray for his wellbeing. So it was, however, with pitiable Mr Edwards'. Some might have thought it a pitiable situation not just for Mr Edwards but for everybody concerned.

Discipline in the Ranks
The real issue at stake here, the cause of which Mr Edwards, the Presbytery of Strathbogie and the decent folk of Marnoch were all alike the unhappy victims, was well brought out in the charges preferred against the offending ministers. By applying to the civil courts for interdict they had denied the truth of God's Holy Word and had disowned the Lord Jesus Christ; contrary to their solemn vows they had acknowledged powers vested by Christ in Church officers alone to be vested in a civil court and had acknowledged the said civil court to be supreme in matters spiritual. It did not even need a vote in the Assembly — the seven were deposed from the ministry on the nod. They had by now a well-trodden path to Parliament House, so thither they hied themselves to seek suspension of sentence and interdict against appointments being made to their parishes. This was granted, the interdict being served on the Assembly while it was still in session. Never had the Kirk been subjected to such indignity.

The extent to which the Kirk was now torn apart by internal strife was well illustrated at the opening of the next Assembly. The deposed majority of Strathbogie Presbytery had sent up two ministers and an elder as, if they were still the Presbytery as they claimed, they were entitled to do. It is said one minister declared the Assembly could not have been worse insulted had the commission come from seven tinkers or scavengers of Edinburgh — a clear enough indication of how tempers were rising. The minority had also sent up commissioners though interdicted from doing so. It was, of course, the latter who were admitted. Whereupon protest was taken that the Assembly was not a legal court and that all their actings would be null and void. Such was the sorry pass in which the supreme court of the Kirk found itself.

Not only the dissenting ministers of Strathbogie were banned, their sympathisers suffered a like fate. No fewer than

11 ministers were accused of having received communion at the hands of their deposed brethren and were in consequence suspended for nine months from the exercise of their judicial functions — which meant they were barred from both the Assembly and their Presbyteries.

But this Assembly of 1842 had business on its hand more pressing than sorting out its membership. For one thing it found by a large majority that patronage was 'a grievance ... the main cause of the evils in which the Church is involved' and that it ought to be abolished. But while patronage was undoubtedly a grievance, and a serious one at that, what had brought so much evil upon the Kirk had been the high-handed way in which she had tried to deal with the matter. If you insist on driving into a lamp-standard you are not entitled to say that the existence of the standard is the principal cause of the damage to your car.

Even more important than this resolution about patronage was the Claim of Right, brought up as an overture and designed as an appeal to the government for redress. This lengthy document began from the headship of Christ and the spiritual freedom of the Kirk, declared the Patronage Act a violation of the Act of Security, claimed that Parliament was now encroaching on the sphere of the Kirk's proper jurisdiction, promised that this would be resisted, and intimated that all legislation affecting the government and discipline of the Church passed without her consent was null and void. The Lord High Commissioner was requested to lay before the Queen the Claim of Right and the Petition on Patronage, and this he undertook to do.

The Assembly also found time to deal with a minister who had challenged the legality of the Chapels Act. This minister had been libelled by his Presbytery for incurring debt and in course of the case had applied to the Court of Session for interdict on the ground that the courts which tried him were vitiated by the presence of the Chapel ministers. He was cited to the bar and summarily deposed from the ministry, not for having contracted debt but for having gone to the secular courts for protection.

Disruption

By the following spring three things had occurred whose

combined effect was to make a parting of the ways inescapable. The first of these was the decision of the House of Lords in the Second Auchterarder Case. It will be recalled that the Presbytery, on Assembly direction, had said that Mr Young was welcome to the stipend of Auchterarder so long as he did not attempt to minister to the people of Auchterarder. The House of Lords resolved unanimously that this would not do, and the Presbytery would have to take Mr Young on trials, or pay him damages.

The second factor was the discovery that in response to the appeal made to the sovereign a dusty answer was likely to be received. Sir James Graham, Secretary of State for the Home Department, it was learned, had echoed the words of the Lord High Commissioner — 'that if to transmit the documents implied the adoption of their sentiments he would have felt it his duty to decline to transmit, but as they related to grievances and were couched in respectful terms he was unwilling to intercept them'. Obviously no help was to be expected from this quarter.

The third deciding factor was an incident which came rather out of the blue. As mentioned above the year 1839 saw the return into the Kirk of the Auld Licht Burghers. Among these was a congregation in Stewarton which had just completed building itself a kirk in the village and whose minister was Mr James Cleland. The charge was welcomed and erected into a parish *quoad sacra*, Mr Cleland was enrolled as a member of the Presbytery of Irvine, and a parish area was in process of being assigned — all in terms of the Chapels Act. It would seem that Cunningham of Lainshaw, the local laird, did not like having the parish of which he was the principal heritor carved up in this way and raised a successful action in the Courts. The Presbytery resolved to contest the judgment, which it did and on 20 January 1843 the decision of the Inner House was intimated — by eight to five it had been found that the Church had no power to create parishes *quoad sacra* or to admit their ministers to membership of the Church courts. So the Chapels Act too was illegal and the *quoad sacra* ministers had no right to sit in the courts. And all on the say-so of a majority in a secular court.

A large-scale secession was inevitable, and, as we all know, it duly occurred, no fewer than 451 ministers walking out of the Establishment, in almost every case at enormous personal sacrifice. The Disruption, no longer a threat, had become a fact.

For our present purpose the only interest in the Disruption is to trace the causes which led to it. Large-scale incidents played their part, but, as we all know, it is personal feelings, prejudices and passions that often count for most in determining the course of human history. Dr Norman MacLeod, who was there at the time, wrote in his diary on 2 June:

> I have returned from the Assembly of 1843, one which will be famous in the annals of the Church of Scotland. Yet who will ever know its real history? The great movements, the grand results, will certainly be known, and everything has been done in the way most calculated to tell on posterity (for how many have been acting before its eyes!); but who in the next century will know or understand the 10 000 influences, the vanity and pride of some, the love of applause, the fear and terror of others, and above all the seceding mania, the revolutionary mesmerism, which I have witnessed within these few days. It was impossible to watch the progress of this schism without seeing that it was inevitable. To pass and to maintain at all hazards laws which by the highest authority were declared to be inconsistent with and subversive of civil statutes could end only in breaking up the Establishment.... Never did I pass such a fortnight of care and anxiety. Never did men engage on a task with more oppression of spirit than we did, as we tried to preserve this Church for the benefit of our children's children.

It is indeed a most enlightening view from the inside.

The Cardross Case

Many and varied were doubtless the motives that inspired the company which walked out of the Establishment on that May day in 1843, but on one thing they enjoyed complete unanimity — they were moving into a realm where they would make and operate their own laws, free from presentations, interdicts, claims for damages and all other forms of outside interference and dictation. How pathetically wrong they were had still to be revealed.

It was 15 years after the Disruption that Mr James MacMillan, first minister of the Free Church congregation at Cardross, was libelled by his Presbytery on a charge of misconduct. Only part of the charge was found proven, and MacMillan took this part of the case to the Synod which upheld his appeal. The Presbytery, however, appealed to the Assembly. Unfortunately the members of the supreme court had put into their hands the print of the entire proceedings, and, in face of protest, they re-opened the whole libel, finding him guilty on charges on which he had already tholed his assize and been acquitted in the lower court. The Assembly suspended him from office *sine die* and loosed him from his charge. Obviously a patrimonial interest was at stake so MacMillan raised an action in the Court of Session, which served an interdict on the Free Church Assembly. That mightily affronted and indignant body immediately cited the offender, confined its hearing to confirming that he had authorised the approach to the civil court, and thereupon deposed him from the ministry of the Free Church. He raised an action for the reduction of the two sentences and for payment of damages.

This, the First Cardross Case, established once and for all that in the eyes of the law the Free Church was a voluntary association on all fours with a football supporters' club or a literary society, and that any member who felt he had been unjustly treated had a remedy in the civil courts. There was only one body in the land to which this did not apply, and that was the Established Kirk. The opinion of Lord Deas has been often quoted in this context:

> Now, if anything be clear in the case, it is that the defenders are invested with no jurisdiction whatever, ecclesiastical or civil. All jurisdiction flows from the supreme power of the State. The sanction of the same authority which enacted the laws is necessary to the erection of the courts, and the appointment of judges and magistrates to administer the laws. The Established Church of Scotland had, and has, this sanction. The statute law of the land conferred upon it ecclesiastical jurisdiction .... But there is no such statute law applicable to the association called the Free Church. When the defenders separated from the Establishment, they left all jurisdiction behind them.[1]

From the lawyer's point of view the Cardross Case was unfortunate in that it dragged on into three cases, one after the other, until MacMillan grew weary — or more likely impoverished — and withdrew from the fray, thus leaving many nice points of law unresolved. From the point of view of the Free Church the case was disastrous, for, as far as they were concerned, it resolved one thing only too clearly — when they separated from the Establishment they left all jurisdiction behind them.

It would be difficult indeed to overestimate the good which was achieved because of the Disruption. In terms of religion it brought a great evangelical revival to the whole of Scotland; in terms of providing the ordinances of religion in a day of population upheaval it made a massive contribution to Church Extension. It is very sad, though, to recognise that the one objective for which the Kirk was split was never realised — the Kirk just cannot be sole judge in the way for which the Popular Party had been clamouring.

The Free Church Case

An important case — some would say the most important case — was still to come, and that half-a-century later.

It had now been accepted that where a secular interest was involved the courts of the realm would claim *locus standi*; but in the matter of a creed, for example, the area was spiritual in character and the ecclesiastical courts could expect to be left to get on with a job which no one could deny was their job alone. It is a fact of life, however, that the temporal and the spiritual cannot be shut away in neat non-communicating compartments — every spiritual experience has to find expression in things that are temporal, and the most secular activity has its spiritual overtones. A very clear example of this overlap is seen in the ownership by a religious body of heritable property. A group of people come together to form a congregation of a certain denomination, they subscribe towards the erection of a church which is then vested in trustees for behoof of the congregation — or is it for behoof of the cause? Think back for a moment to the days of the Auld Lichts an' a' that — what is to happen to the property when the inevitable split occurs, should it go with the majority or should it stay with the minority who abide faithful to the principles for the promulgation of which the building had been put up in the first place? The 19th century, naturally, saw many cases go to the courts.

The civil courts were, understandably, unwilling to become too deeply involved. For one thing they probably did not want to appear to be intruding into a territory which should be the preserve of Presbyteries and General Assemblies; and for another thing they almost certainly felt very much at sea amid the complexities of the denominational controversies of those days.

A case arose in 1801 concerning the minister of a Burgher cause in Aberdeen who, not content with adopting New Licht ideas, fixed new locks to the kirk doors to keep out the majority of the congregation who had remained Auld Licht and had retained the auld keys. In the case which ensued this interesting pronouncement was made: 'The court cannot enter into an investigation as to the religious grounds of the schism here, and if they did, they must assume the majority to be right.'

Another property case, that of Craigdallie, was in and out of the courts for 20 years before it finally emerged from the House of Lords with the doctrine clearly enunciated 'that property is held in trust for the principles of the Church'.[2] This sounds good, and even simple, but it is going to have two interesting repercussions — first that a Church is going to be gravely hampered if in the exercise of its vaunted freedom to formulate and interpret its standards, it is putting the ownership of its property at risk; and secondly the courts of the realm, which have the duty of settling questions relating to ownership of property, are going to find themselves acting as judges on issues which at least appear to be wholly spiritual issues. Is there to be no end to the interference of the secular courts?

It was precisely this question of the relation between the ownership of property and adherence to religious principles that lay at the heart of the famous Free Church Case which was finally issued by the House of Lords in 1904. The United Presbyterian Church, it will be recalled, united with the Free Church in 1900 to form the United Free Church, but quite a strong minority on the Free Church side opted out. The ministers of this minority were solemnly deposed and actions were raised for recovery of the property they were occupying. This, naturally, was resisted. The plea of the Wee Frees, as they came to be called, was that in two respects those of their number who had entered the union had abandoned Free Church principles — first in departing from the principle of a National Establishment of Religion, which was a fundamental tenet of the Free Church, in order to adopt a Voluntaryism which stemmed from the Secession; and secondly in departing from that rigid adherence to the Westminster Confession, which was a fundamental tenet of the Free Church, in order to adopt the new United Free attitude to the Confession, which left people free to adopt either of two interpretations.

Judgment was given in favour of the Free Church. This created a quite outrageous situation, the thirty remaining congregations of the Free Church having acquired the whole heritable property of that body, which they could not even administer, let alone use or maintain. As we all know, Parliament intervened and in 1905, in the interests of justice, set up a Commission to allocate the property on a fair and equitable basis.

This ends the tale of the conflict between the courts of the Kirk and the courts of the Kingdom, and a remarkable conclusion we appear to have reached. On the Kirk side a minority left the Establishment because of what they saw as outside interference in matters where alone the Lord Jesus Christ was King, only to find themselves in a worse position than they had left. One might think the Kirk did not emerge with great credit. But on the other side the supreme civil judicatory of the land issued a judgment which was no doubt impeccable law but which bore so little relation to reality that a Commission had to be appointed to sort out the resulting mess in a way that would achieve justice. Perhaps one might also think the courts did not cover themselves with glory either.

But, glory or no glory, the round was won by the courts of the realm.

References
1 MacMillan v The General Assembly of the Free Church of Scotland (1859) 22 D 290.
2 Davidson v Aikman (1805) Mor 14584.

VI

The Contemporary Kirk

Re-union in 1929
It would be reasonable to regard the contemporary Kirk as dating from 1929, for it was in October of that year that, after long and earnest preparation, the United Free Church of Scotland and the Church of Scotland joined to form what can properly be described as a new, or at least a renewed, Church of Scotland. The body which emerged at that time can be said to represent an almost complete re-union of all the shattered fragments into which in these chapters we have witnessed the Kirk of the Scottish Reformation being broken.

Unhappily there were those on the former United Free side who did not see their way to come in and who continued — and who continue to this day — as a separate denomination. The Wee Frees (those of the Free Church who had not united in 1900) and the Free Presbyterians, a group which left the Free Church in 1892 when liberty of opinion was permitted in relation to the Westminster Confession — these two denominations still offer their independent testimony and attract a considerable following, mainly in the West Highlands and in the Islands. The Cameronian tradition is faithfully kept alive in the Reformed Presbyterian Church which has a number of congregations in the Covenanting southwest. Various Auld Licht groups which had resisted unions of one sort or another finally came together to form the United Original Secession Church, and in 1954 this body, small but hardy, acceded to the Church of Scotland. It can be said then with some confidence that the Church of Scotland is today the national Church, and that not merely in a legal or constitutional sense but in the sense that it is the Kirk of the great majority of the people of Scotland, having on its rolls the names of about 25 per cent of the adult population and commanding the allegiance of a vast number more.

It would be a mistake to imagine that the Union of 1929 resulted in the immediate disappearance of differences or in a completely harmonious interlocking of systems. Changes and accommodations had to be made in the interest of unity and as always there were diehards — on both sides — who saw in these the certain prelude to disaster. There is a lovely tale of a dyed-in-the-wool Auld Kirk minister who had occasion to visit the offices of the united Church, these being the former United Free premises. There was a lift, temperamental in character, of the old-fashioned variety with a metal grille frame. As was to be expected, the lift chose the occasion of having our Auld Kirk friend as its guest to play one of its pranks and get stuck between floors. The rescuers were much diverted to find the exasperated occupant rattling the gates and demanding in a loud voice, 'Will somebody get me out of this damned UF contrivance!'

Congregational Readjustment

Apart from the many difficulties at the personal and human level inevitably connected with a union on so vast a scale, there was one very challenging problem confronting the new body — that of readjusting its congregations. We have noted how the Secessions and the Disruption helped to meet the demand for religious ordinances stemming from the population explosion of earlier days. The result of this was that there were generally three Presbyterian congregations in every parish in the land. There was the former Parish Church, situated usually near the geographical centre of the parish and often quite remote from the main centre of population; there was the Free Church, almost certainly in the heart of the town or village; and there was the former UP cause whose geographical location depended upon a variety of interesting historical factors. By 1929 Scotland was facing rapid depopulation of its rural areas, and in most cases one church would have sufficed where there were three. People all agreed with this proposition so long as it related to some parish other than their own. But over the years personal jealousies and animosities have a way of creeping in and taking the place of doctrinal differences that have been outlived, and the readjusting of agencies which on paper can appear so simple is discovered on the ground to be bitter, complicated, and near impossible to achieve.

The Kirkmabreck Case

On the east shore of Wigtown Bay, looking across to the spot where the martyrs met their cruel fate, lies the Parish of Kirkmabreck, famous for the granite quarried at Carsluith. In 1934 when the Presbytery tried to effect a union between the old Parish congregation of Kirkmabreck and the former United Free congregation of Creetown they were met with a spirit as thrawn as the Covenanters and as hard as the local stone. Negotiations there were a-plenty, but progress none. While all this talking was going on both congregations, naturally, had had progress in their vacancies sisted. In 1936 a group of elders in the former Parish Church raised an action against the Presbytery, claiming that the right to elect a minister was a civil right conferred upon them by statute, in the Act of 1874 (the one that finally abolished patronage) and that they were being wrongfully prevented from the exercise of that right.

The case went to the Second Division of the Court of Session which by a majority of two to one found in favour of the Presbytery. For the Kirk this is a crucial judgment. The issue that was before the court was quite simply that of interpreting the Articles Declaratory. If the provisions of the 1921 Act were as comprehensive as they appeared then the matter of calling a minister was a spiritual matter and lay wholly within the jurisdiction of the Church courts. As the Lord Justice Clerk, Craigie Aitchison, put it in his leading opinion:

> The question must therefore be, Is the particular matter complained of ... a matter which, on a reasonable construction, falls within the Declaratory Articles? If so the matter is at an end, and neither the statute, nor the common law, nor previous judicial decision, whether upon statute or upon common law, can avail to bring the matter within the jurisdiction of the civil authority.

He had no difficulty in finding on a reasonable construction that the right to call was a matter falling within the scope of the Articles Declaratory and consequently falling outwith the jurisdiction of his court.[1]

It is very important to note that both sides agreed that it lay within the province of the Court of Session to determine whether the matter fell within its domain — that is to say, the Kirk conceded that Caesar should be judge of what belongs to Caesar and what belongs to God — a position vastly different from that adopted by the Popular Party prior to 1843.

With, then, this concession on the part of the Kirk — if one may see it in that light — the position has now been judicially established that in all matters which in view of the civil courts are spiritual matters the Kirk herself is to be sole judge. It is perhaps unfortunate that the case was not taken farther, for, as I indicated, it was a majority decision of two to one and Lord Mackay's minority opinion is a forceful and cogent one. But there it stands and the Kirk can rest content to leave it so.

Revolt in the Ranks
During the time the readjustment negotiations were making heavy weather at Kirkmabreck one might have overheard on the streets of Creetown someone declaring, 'We're no' goin' to be dictated to by the Presbytery!' At Kirkmabreck in fact once the case had gone against the elders negotiations were resumed and in due course a union was effected. It has not always been so, however, for there is within the Kirk a fairly widespread spirit of congregationalism. However much lip-service is paid to conciliar government the congregation is seen as entitled in the last resort to make up its own mind on its own future. From time to time since 1929, and invariably over some question of readjustment, we have seen a congregation seceding from the Kirk. In every instance, so far as I know, the seceders have been accepted into some other denomination, generally the Congregational Union, though on occasion the United Free Church. In such a case a vital question arises as to the ownership of buildings. Generally nowadays all property is vested in the General Trustees or is held for behoof of the Church of Scotland and therefore cannot be alienated by a seceding congregation. But there have been cases where the congregation was formerly UP and was in a position to take its property with it.

It is one thing for a group of congregations to detach

THE CONTEMPORARY KIRK

themselves from the mainstream of the Kirk's life and create a new denomination, but one solitary congregation obviously cannot do this. The consequence is that the seceding congregation becomes a congregational church, and whether or not it allies itself with the Congregational Union is a quite separate question. An intriguing situation was created south of the border in 1972 when the Presbyterian Church of England united with the Congregational Union of England and Wales to form the United Reformed Church of England and Wales. A large body of congregations from the latter Church stayed out of the union, and since they were independent units no problem arose for them in doing this. A number of congregations on the Presbyterian side were unhappy at the prospect of the union, but what could such a congregation do? It seemed that the only way in which it could express its antipathy to the idea of congregationalism was by itself becoming a congregational church. Scarcely the happiest solution! Which probably explains why, with the single exception of Wallace Green in Berwick-on-Tweed — which was a quite exceptional case and successfully petitioned for admission to the Church of Scotland — all the others entered the union.

Decision-Making

The claim not to be dictated to by the Presbytery is a perhaps regrettable symptom of a growing spirit of independency that can be detected among our congregations. This is a natural enough reaction to the contemporary trend to remove decision-making in more and more departments of congregational life from the local level to some faraway place about which the congregation knows little but fears the worst.

Let us take stipend as an example, and let us consider the case of a former UP congregation, descendants of the folk who battled their ferocious way through Burgher and New Licht controversies. Until comparatively recent times — say, the last 40 years — the amount to be paid each year as stipend was fixed by the congregation at their annual meeting (at which, incidentally, the minister was not present) and was paid to him direct by the Treasurer, three months in advance, be it said. In this way, the UPs maintained, they were able to recognise and reward diligence and success, and also —

though they might not say so much about this — they were able to determine the income of the minister in the light not of his needs or his deserts, but on the condition of the congregational finances — 'the minister should really have been getting a rise but we've been faced with a big bill for repairs to the roof.' The peace of this long-established system was rudely disturbed by the appearance in the wake of the Union of 1929 of the Vacancy Schedule, a document setting forth the stipend which was to be paid and the amount of aid that was to be given to, or to be received from, the Minimum Stipend Fund. This Schedule had to be completed by the Managers in conference with representatives of the Presbytery and had to receive the imprimatur of the Presbytery and of the Assembly Committee on the Maintenance of the Ministry before a new minister could be inducted. The decision-making had been moved from the congregation to the Managers in conference with the Presbytery. Then in 1952 under the guidance of the late Karl Greenlaw the idea of the Appropriate Stipend made its appearance. The operative principle here was that a list was drawn up showing what in all the circumstances of each congregation was a stipend appropriate to be paid by that body. This list, prepared by the Presbytery, had to be approved by the Edinburgh Committee, but not, be it noted, by the congregations concerned. So the decision-making had now passed out of the hands of the local members altogether. The Treasurer, however, had still the satisfaction of handing over to the minister his monthly cheque. Or so it was until 1975 since when each stipend is paid direct into the bank account of the minister concerned by the Office in Edinburgh. All that is left for the erstwhile decision-makers is to collect and forward the money. Let us be fair and admit that in today's world of Pay-As-You-Earn, National Insurance, Pension Fund contributions and all the rest there is a great deal to be said in defence of the new system, and certainly it would be admitted on all hands that it works admirably. But the price that has to be paid is the removal of all initiative and decision-making from the local people who put up the money, with all the weakening of interest and the creation of discontent to which that must necessarily lead.

It is basically the same story with regard to giving to the

Schemes of the Church. I can clearly remember a day when the needs of the Schemes were met by 'retiring collections' — and I can remember the howl of laughter that greeted John White's sally in the Assembly that they were often 'very retiring'! On the other side it has to be said that in those days congregations had their pet schemes to which they contributed, often until it hurt. Then in 1961 the Co-ordinated Appeal came along and congregations found themselves assessed for a lump sum which would be divided up in ways over which they had no control. A system of free-will giving replaced with a system of taxation, the decision being reached by people devoid of faces — or so at least it was easy for the cynics to complain.

It is the system that creates the cynics and their numbers are inclining to increase, so that one can envisage a day when there might be congregational revolt over financial matters. This may not lead readily to secession, perhaps just to withholding the monthly remittance! But one thing has a way of leading to another, and once the spirit of revolt is in the air there is no saying where it may end.

Democracy in the Kirk

All of this leads inevitably to the question of just how democratic is our system of Church government at congregational level. And the short answer is that there is only one thing in the life of a congregation that is completely democratic, and that is the choosing of a minister to fill a vacancy. Bearing in mind the anguish that had to be endured by many generations ere this right of choice was won, it is not surprising that it should be treasured. In its actual operation the business of choosing is a bit messy, but then democracy is always a bit messy — while tyranny can be counted on to be neat and tidy. And it works as well as any other kind of electing. Considering how little freedom of choice the congregation is going to enjoy once the minister is inducted it is understandable that they should have a bit of a ball while he is still being chosen!

This business of free unrestricted choice is deeply worrying. It means a lot to congregations, but how long can it be continued in this modern day and how soon may we need to have recourse to some form of direction? We are living in an age of change — never were the words of the ancient philosopher more apposite, *panta rhei*, all things flow. Time was when there was some degree of stability about our social structures and it was a reasonable thing to anchor a man in a parish *ad vitam aut culpam*, but that day is passing, if it has not already gone. In Glasgow, for example, we have seen instances where a busy, bustling, thriving parish was converted into a sea of red blaes within a matter of, say, ten years. What in these circumstances does the security of tenure represented by *ad vitam aut culpam* mean to a minister? It is becoming more and more apparent that the courts of the Church must be given power to take men out of certain situations and it must be evident that that power to move a man out will avail little unless accompanied by a corresponding power to move a man in. If for a moment I may assume the mantle of the prophet I should say the day is coming, and may not be far distant, when we shall have to devise a much more fluid and moveable pattern of ministry, and just how this is to be done while at the same time preserving the democratic right of the congregation to choose should provide an engrossing study for tomorrow's Churchmen.

Courts versus Committees
Still on the subject of democratic rights, a very interesting question is raised by the tension that sometimes appears between courts and committees — meaning, of course, Standing Committees of the General Assembly. From time to time a Presbytery and an Edinburgh Committee find themselves at loggerheads and harsh things tend to be said — always about the Committee. To understand properly the position it is helpful to know something of the history of our Committee structure.

The first thing to realise is that when Presbyterianism was initially established the work of the Kirk in Scotland was confined within the parishes of Scotland, and Kirk Sessions, Presbyteries, Synods, and General Assemblies were adequate to cope with all its activities. It was a parish-centred system and the superior courts functioned mainly as courts of appeal. It was when the Kirk began to see herself as having obligations in the world beyond her parishes, beyond Scotland's shore, that the system could not cope and something had to be done. When, for example, the passion for overseas mission laid hold upon the Kirk, somebody had to be appointed to take charge of a business which, apart from being financially supported by them, had no connection whatever with the parishes. So the Assembly appointed a Committee of their own number to do the job. Naturally, as the wider work of the Kirk developed the number of these Committees increased. Inevitably too as the system expanded the power and influence of the Committee grew. They are answerable only to the General Assembly, and as there is a long time between one Assembly and the next the Committee must be accorded a considerable freedom to act on its own authority, even if at the end of the day it has to receive Assembly endorsement of what has been done. Always, though, when the Assembly has given a remit to a Committee it has had in mind the powers of the courts and has written in provisions to protect their position. The result is a system of balances and counter-balances, and the fact that there can be this occasional confrontation between court and committee is a sign of health rather than of weakness. It is just not true to say — as is sometimes done — that the Kirk is becoming a bureaucracy run by a small group of people at 121 George Street whose main characteristic is a delusion of grandeur.

It is a pity this kind of thing should be said, much more that it should be believed. Church government is, as it has always been, the preserve of the courts, the business of the Committees being strictly executive and administrative. Obviously these two aspects are not always clear-cut or easy to differentiate. The same kind of tension is to be seen at the national level when on occasion a Ministry arrogates to itself an authority properly belonging to Parliament alone. That these Ministries are keen not to be thought to be trespassing in this way is evidenced by the speed with which the threat of a question on the floor of the House will bring to heel even the most arrogant Ministry. In like fashion the Committees of the Kirk have always shown a distinct disinclination to join issue with a court at the bar of the Assembly. Correctly operated the Committee system offers no threat to the power of Presbyteries as courts of the Kirk. Bureaucracy can only supplement, it can never supplant Presbyterianism.

The real worry about the growth of the Edinburgh Committee system is the way in which it discourages initiative at the grass roots. We have already commented upon how this has occurred in the sphere of finance. Not so apparent, but far more serious, is its development at the spiritual level. The original conception of Presbyterianism provided for initiative being taken at the perimeter — in the parishes that is — and moving towards the centre one passed through a series of courts of appeal whose business it was to keep track of what was going forward and to ensure that no-one got too far out of line. It is a totally modern idea that the Assembly from its Committees through the Presbyteries should send down directives to ministers, kirk sessions, and congregations. Looking up for directives — what might be called the civil service mentality — is a phenomenon of modern times and is utterly foreign to true Presbyterianism and sadly to the loss of the Kirk. It used to be that a Kirk Session went ahead and did something, confident that the superior courts would pull it up if it transgressed; today it does nothing till the Assembly sends it instructions. I have had a minister come to discuss with me some bright idea he has had for the improvement of the work in his parish and I have said to him, 'That's a splendid idea; off you go and get on with it.' He has looked horrified and explained that all he was doing was making a suggestion which he thought some Assembly Committee might care to take up. The unused limb becomes atrophied. If we in the lower courts refuse to avail ourselves of the enormous power that Presbyterianism puts in our hand because we want the protection and shelter of a chit from the office upstairs then we cannot wonder, and have no right to complain, if we see a massive bureaucracy building up on top of a Presbyterianism that is quite unsuited to carry it.

To sum up on this aspect of things: looked at theoretically, there could appear to be a threat to Presbyterian Church government posed by the relentless growth of the Committee system; but looked at as a practical proposition I do not believe the danger to be very great — and that for two reasons. First — and it is easy to overlook this — the personnel of the courts and the committees is identical. It may appear that some peculiar miasma descends upon a man as he crosses the portals of '121', but not, I think, sufficient to render him unaware of his responsibilities towards the court which in most cases he is supposed to be representing. And second that so long as there are still those in our pulpits and, even more important, in our pews in whose veins there still courses the blood of Covenanter, Anti-Burgher and Non-Intrusionist we may rest confident the Assembly will be constantly alerted to keep a tight rein on Committees which, after all, are her own creatures.

Ecumenical Bodies

Not from within is Presbyterianism threatened, but from without. So by way of conclusion I turn to a quite different subject, to a consideration of how the Kirk's claim to be mistress in her own household is affected by what is one of the most significant features of the Church's life in this generation, the growth of ecumenism. In earlier chapters we saw how the passion for conscience and separation shattered the unity of the Kirk in the 18th century. 'Shattered the unity of the Kirk' — not 'shattered the Kirk'; for there has probably never been a time when the Kirk has had a stronger hold upon the allegiance of the people of the land than in the days of the Auld Lichts an' a' that. In this latter half of the 20th century we have moved to the opposite extreme, and the period since the 1930s has been marked by endless discussion about Church unity, and about Church union. Almost invariably these have tended to be equated though this I believe to be quite misleading. In these islands during the period in question there has been very little actual union achieved, but there has been talk, conference, debate and, more important, there has been a readiness to work together, and even to worship together. The period has been characterised too by the growth of what for want of a better term I call ecumenical bodies.

Let us examine three of these, in reverse order of seniority. There is the World Council of Churches, an institution founded as recently as 1948 by the fusion of the Commissions on Faith and Order and on Life and Work, an organisation that has positively mushroomed in recent years with now over two hundred member churches. It defines itself as 'a fellowship of Christians who confess the Lord Jesus Christ as God and Saviour and therefore seek to fulfil their common calling to the glory of God, Father, Son, and Holy Spirit.'

To me this has always seemed a strange charter. Why the 'therefore' — no obvious train of logical thought is disclosed but only an assertion made. And what of 'their common calling'? Is that not a begging of the question? Should not the charter spell out for us precisely what that common calling is? Secondly there is the British Council of Churches, dating from 1942 and involving 16 denominations within these shores. And finally the World Alliance of Reformed Churches, dating from as early as 1875 when 21 Reformed and Presbyterian denominations sent delegates to London where they agreed to form what was then called 'The Alliance of Reformed Churches Throughout the World Holding the Presbyterian System.' There are others but these are sufficient for my purpose.

These bodies, especially the two Councils, have developed into organisations of considerable size, employing fairly large staffs that include many ordained personnel, and having budgets running into very large figures. They are not Churches, for they do not minister to a single soul, but they concern themselves deeply in public questions of various kinds, such as race relations, industrial disputes, the third world, women's rights — all in addition to advancing the cause of ecumenism. On these and other like issues they make public pronouncements, they publish books, they second personnel to work in affected areas. In order that a Church should become a member of one of these organisations all that is required, so far as I know, is that it should satisfy the Council that it is a genuine Christian Church and that it is prepared to pay a kind of membership fee scaled according to its size — though even this may sometimes be waived. It then acquires a right to be represented on the Council and its representatives may in due course be chosen to act on some of the many departmental committees, commissions, and so on.

The question which immediately presents itself to my mind is, how far does membership of, say, the World Council commit an independent denomination to the policies and to the pronouncements of the World Council? I think that the answer must emphatically be: Not at all. Yet it is very difficult for the individual Church, however much it may wish to do so, to dissociate itself from the acts and utterances of a body of which it is known to be a constituent part. The problem arose very sharply a number of years ago when the World Council in its campaign to combat racism resolved to make grants to political groups in emergent countries which were openly committed to a policy of violence. Originally it was proposed to give money held in a building reserve, and this would almost certainly have been a misuse of trust funds. In the event a special fund was set up to receive specific contributions and to make grants. If a body like the World Council cares to act as intermediary in conveying to those involved at the receiving end the contributions of those member Churches who wish to be associated in an effort of this controversial kind, it is fulfilling a proper function; but if without specific authorisation monies which the Church of Scotland gave for the general work of the Council are used then the Church is being committed to the support of a cause to which it may well be, and indeed was proved to be, utterly hostile. If we put the Council in a position where it can do that kind of thing then we are to that extent surrendering our sovereignty — we are no longer sole judge.

Greatly daring, I should say that the World Council suffers from two fundamental weaknesses. The first of these is that it is too far removed from the man in the pew. It has come to forget that he exists, or at least to imagine that he is not its concern — not at least until the time comes for the balancing of the finances. It is tragically easy for this to happen. For one thing the Council is not itself a Church and has no pews for men to occupy; for another, the delegates who constitute its membership are predominantly people who in their own denominations occupy administrative and other similar posts far removed from the rank and file of the Church membership; and for yet another, many of the themes that occupy the Council are beyond the normal range of interest of the man in the pew. Discussion and debate take place in a rarefied atmosphere. The fact that so much surprise was engendered by the storm of protest that greeted the proposal to give aid to violent minorities was clear evidence of this chasm of separation. Admitted we have need of leaders, and a leader has to be out in front, but it is a conviction of mine that when a leader has got so far in front as to have lost contact with the troops he is no longer a leader, he has become a deserter.

And the second weakness affecting a body like the World Council is the temptation to see itself as a kind of super-Church when, in fact, as noted above, it is not a Church at all. I remember after a visit to the offices in Geneva saying I felt I had seen something between the United Nations and the Vatican — if on a slightly smaller scale. Hence the temptation to make pronouncements, particularly at the international level. Now, as I see it, it is not for the Council to speak *for* the Churches, its job is to speak *to* the Churches. It has no mandate to pass judgments in the name of the Churches — we in the Kirk have never handed over our right to reach our own conclusions on these issues and to take such steps thereanent as may to us seem proper. What the Council can do — what it is outstandingly well qualified to do — is to examine some burning issue, tease it out, marshal all the facts, indicate the implications, go on if it will to say what action it thinks is called for by Christian Churches in such a situation, and then leave it to the Churches to react in the way which to them seems right and proper. Anything more than this is an interference with our autonomy — and our fathers at least had a way of dealing with that kind of thing.

If the Kirk is to retain her position as sole judge in all matters pertaining to her polity then, as I see it, some quite serious thought needs to be given to the role of the ecumenical bodies with which we are associated and with the nature and extent of that association.

The Ecumenical Movement

So much for the ecumenical bodies: what of the ecumenical movement generally? The enthusiasts for ecumenism keep reminding us of the Seventh Declaratory Article where the Kirk 'recognises the obligation to seek and promote union with other Churches'. What is not so often quoted is the reservation that these are to be Churches in which the Kirk is satisfied that 'the Word is being purely preached, the Sacraments administered according to Christ's ordinance, and discipline rightly exercised.' The discipline here referred to is not the kind of moral supervision of the conduct of parishioners so assiduously exercised by Kirk Sessions of yesteryear, but is simply Church government in general. And the crucial question is whether or not we of the Presbyterian tradition can, while remaining true to that tradition and retaining our identity, agree that an Episcopal Church measures up to this requirement. I very much doubt it.

Should we be so minded I am sure we have the power ourselves to become an Episcopal Church. What to me is equally clear is that we are not free at one and the same time to adopt Episcopacy and retain our contract with the State represented by the Act of 1921, nor indeed to claim the protection of the Act of Security — would it not be a droll situation were we to require of the sovereign an oath to defend inviolate in Scotland a Presbyterianism from which we ourselves had deliberately departed?

It is true, that Article I — the unalterable Article — speaks only about what the Kirk believes and says nothing about how she is to be governed. Article II, however, affirms bluntly enough that the government of the Church is Presbyterian and is exercised through Kirk Sessions, Presbyteries, Provincial Synods and General Assemblies, and while it makes provision for this to be 'interpreted or modified by Acts of Assembly or by consuetude' it makes no provision whatever for it to be abandoned altogether — by Act of Assembly or by any other method. When, a few years ago, the suggestion was made that the Synod had outlived its usefulness as a court of the Church there were those who strongly contended that Article II made it impossible for the Synod to be scrapped. The issue was never put to the test, and for my own part I should support the view that the Synod could go out without loss of our Presbyterian identity. I am not at all satisfied that a Bishop could come in without loss of our Presbyterian identity.

Let us for a moment allow our imagination to make a real flight of fancy. Let us suppose that we had reached the stage of being prepared to accept Episcopacy and were committed to an incorporating union with the Church of England which involved our accepting bishops, what would happen within the field wherein our present interest lies — how far would such a Church be sole judge? If our experience with our southern neighbour in other walks of life is anything to go by the resulting body would in all likelihood be still the Church of England with us as the 'Northern See'. And in that case possibly the Church–State relationship presently obtaining in England would continue — for what it is worth. If, however, the union resulted in what was genuinely a new creation, a Church of Great Britain, then I imagine a new agreement would have to be worked out with the State, and my guess is that opportunity would be taken to effect a complete disestablishment, to put the Church on a footing similar to that of any other voluntary association. After all — and we could not deny this — our two national Churches were accorded the status they respectively enjoy in a day when they in each case represented what might be called the nation at prayer. The very same people made up the nation as made up the Church. Today that position is completely altered. The Church of Scotland can claim one out of every four of the adult population as enrolled in its membership; the Church of England only a fraction of that. One can hear the politicians argue that the Church should not be continued in a position of privilege which, however relevant three centuries ago, is meaningless today. No doubt also the Roman Catholic Church would be in on the act with a claim for equal status — at least.

Bishop in Presbytery

All of which is very much in the field of conjecture — wild conjecture if you like. But there is no element of speculation about the booklet, *God's Reign and Our Unity: the Report of the Anglican-Reformed Commission 1984*. The Commission responsible for this publication is a body set up by the Anglican Consultative Council and the World Alliance of Reformed Churches, and the Report represents the result of four years of joint study. The Kirk as such was not represented on the conferring body, but members of the Kirk did, I understand, take part in their capacity as delegates from the World Alliance. The book finds that there is a high degree of unity between Anglican and Reformed communions on many subjects, including baptism and the eucharist. On what it admits to be 'the more divisive question' of the nature of the ministry it agrees that the New Testament does not prescribe any specific structure as normative for all time, but it pleads that the threefold ministry of bishop, priest, and deacon, since it was the pattern which eventually prevailed, since it was generally accepted by the Church, and since it has been maintained by the large majority of Churches to the present day, should be adopted in some form. I quote from the Report:

> If our two communions are to become one, Reformed Churches will have to face the question of bishops, Anglican Churches will have to reconsider the question of the diaconate and take into account Reformed experience of the eldership, and both communions will have to take more seriously the role of the whole membership in the governance of the Church.[2]

To digress for a moment, it might be illuminating to comment upon this promise that Anglicans 'will take into account the Reformed experience of the eldership', for the words have a familiar ring. They take us back to the Bishops Report of 1957 which said that 'lay persons would be solemnly "set apart" for some measure of pastoral responsibility towards their fellow-Christians in an office akin to the Presbyterian eldership.' The interesting thing is that in both cases, having thus filed away the Anglican contribution for future reference the Report goes on to pursue with no little diligence the incorporation of Bishops into the Kirk.

In view of the fact that all the possibility amounts to, at best, is that of 'setting apart' as opposed to ordaining, and envisages 'a measure of pastoral responsibility' within the congregation as opposed to the position of rule in every court of the Kirk which is of the essence of the office of elder — considering these reservations even the fulfilment of the promise would do nothing to preserve the essential character of the eldership. And that is every bit as much a feature of Presbyterianism as the historic episcopate is of Anglicanism. The new Church may at some time in the future acquire persons bearing a faint resemblance to elders; but before the new Church gets off the ground it has to get itself equipped with full-blooded Bishops in the Apostolic Succession.

It may seem that I am pursuing a venomous vendetta here. I apologise if that be so, for all I wish is to show how the proposals are bound to lead to the dismemberment of the Presbyterian system, to whose defence we all of us stand committed.

The Bishops Report of 1957 propounded the idea of the Bishop-in-Presbytery. I quote:

> Bishops chosen by each Presbytery, from its own membership or otherwise, would initially be consecrated by prayer with the laying on of hands by bishops from one or more of the Episcopal Churches and by the Presbytery acting through appointed representatives. Thus consecrated each Bishop would be within the Apostolic Succession as acknowledged by Anglicans on the one hand and as required by Presbyterians on the other. He would be the President of the Presbytery and would act as its principal minister in every ordination and in consecration of other Bishops.

The new Report is rather less forceful and the element of the Apostolic Succession is played down. These are to be 'low-key Bishops' — that is to say, we are here dealing with only the thin end of the wedge. What we are to have is just a permanent Moderator of Presbytery. What harm can there be in that? There is nothing revolutionary there. It is precisely here that I want to join issue, for I believe the change to be absolutely revolutionary. I see it as meaning that we abandon our identity and that in consequence it imperils our unique position as sole judge in all our own affairs. Let us look at the proposals in greater detail.

First, the new-style Moderator is to hold office 'for a substantial period' — only so can he become known as representative of the Church in the particular area. Now the whole point of our Presbyterian system is that the Moderator does not stand in any such relation to the charges within the bounds. His relationship is confined, and strictly confined, to the Presbytery at whose meetings he takes the chair and at which he rules on all matters of order. His power is assumed when the meeting is constituted and discarded when the benediction is pronounced — and to keep him mindful of the limited nature of his rule we appoint him for only a year — until the late 1940s it was for only six months.

Second, the new-style Moderator will have to be relieved of other duties in order to fulfil this role. What is envisaged, then, is not a Moderator of Presbytery who will undertake additional duties but a person consecrated for the performance of other duties who will act as President of the

Presbytery. I am glad they call him President, for Moderator he is not.

This point is brought out even more clearly in the third paragraph which says that 'his role would be more than that of presiding at meetings' — he would be 'called to leadership in the whole life of the Church in his area.' Already the great Presbyterian concept of the equality of the ministry is out of the window. Not only so, serious questions are now arising as to the position of the Presbytery itself, a body which had been fondly imagining it enjoyed an overall responsibility for all things spiritual within its bounds.

It is in the fourth paragraph that we come around to the idea of the College of Bishops, though the exact form that this will take is still to be discussed. When you reach this stage it is the authority of the General Assembly that is in jeopardy. It seems to me most unfortunate — at the kindliest estimate — that this crucial matter could not have been discussed and firm proposals framed in course of the four years of talking that have already taken place. This is no optional extra which does not matter very much either way; this lies at the very heart of the matter. When, for example, the moment comes for issuing final judgment on some doctrinal issue, who is to occupy the bench — is it to be the General Assembly or is it to be the College of Bishops? We are entitled to know.

I imagine it would be possible to defend the proposition that in moving from a constantly changing Moderator to a permanent one we are merely 'interpreting or modifying' our Presbyterian form of Church government, though my own opinion is that it would require a fair amount of ingenuity to frame a convincing case. I cannot, however, conceive that the introduction into our system of the Bishop-in-Presbytery depicted in *God's Reign and Our Unity* is anything less than a complete departure from the position to which we committed ourselves in 1921 when we put our name to the Declaratory Articles.

Let it be that the Kirk got around to accepting the proposals of the Report and entered into some kind of incorporating union on the basis of the degree of Episcopacy which is envisaged here. It seems to me certain beyond a peradventure that a minority would protest and separate — if once he gets sufficiently roused, the Scot of today can be as dour as his Auld Licht forebears and (though this never seems to be recognised) there are those with conscientious objections to Apostolic Succession every whit as deeply held as is the conscientious acceptance of the doctrine by others. This remanent body of protesters would undoubtedly sue for the property which is vested in trustees for behoof of a Church whose government is Presbyterian. How easily we could have another Free Kirk case, and how tragic and pathetic and purposeless it would all be. If only those who are so keen to lead us along these paths of ecumenical dalliance would pause and think of the possible consequences. The most complete success in their labours would bring us little real advance in the business of winning Scotland for Christ; it could at the same time bring unspeakable tragedy to the religious life of the Scottish people.

Our studies in the chapters above have shown us, surely, that the position of the Kirk as sole judge in matters spiritual is a prize that has been won by years of struggle, that it is a thing of enormous worth not to be put at needless risk. It could well be said to be one of the brightest ornaments in the Kirk's crown. Let my last word on this last page be a word of warning — in my experience ornaments are delicate things, you just cannot be too careful how you handle them.

References
1 Ballantyne v The Presbytery of Wigtown (1936) SC 625.
2 The Report of the Anglican-Reformed International Commission (1984). *God's Reign and Our Unity*. SPCK/The Saint Andrew Press, London, p72.

Index

Accession Oath 17, 22–23
Act Rescissory 40
Anti-Burghers 74–75, 78, 80–83
Articles Declaratory 8–11, 111, 127
   Article I 123
   Article II 123
   Article IV 9
   Article V 10
   Article VI 11
   Article VII 10, 122
Articles of faith, Five 33, 38
Associate Presbytery 57, 70–71, 82
         Synod 17, 57, 74–75
Auchterarder Case, The first 95–96
              , The second 98, 103
Auchterarder Creed 59–60
Auld Licht Burghers 68ff, 79–80, 82–84, 103

Beaton, David 25
Bishop 30–32, 38, 40, 123–127
   Bishops Report 124–127
Black Acts, The 30–31
Book of Common Order (1564) 27
Book of Common Prayer 35
Book of Metrical Psalms 49–50
Bothwell Brig 41, 43-45
Breach, The 74–75, 85
British Council of Churches 20, 120
Bruce, Archibald 82
bureaucracy 20, 117
Burgess Oath 72–73, 83
burgh churches 91
Burghers 74

call 92
Calvin, John 25

Calvinists 59
Cambuslang wark 71–72
Cameron, Richard 43
Cameronians 44, 71, 109
Cardross Case, The 19, 104–106
Cargill, Donald 43
Catechism 49–50
Chapels Act, The 19, 94–95, 102–103
Chapel of Ease 91
Charles I 16, 33–34, 38
Charles II 40
Church Extension 91–92, 106
Church and State 11–12, 17, 23, 27, 29, 33, 80–84, 124
Claim of Right 22, 102
collegiate charges 91
Covenant, The National 36–37, 40–41, 46, 78
  Covenants 17, 42, 71, 79, 82
  Covenanters 60, 69, 82
conventicle 41–42
Cromwell, Oliver 17, 40

democracy 115–116
Directory of Public Worship 49
Disruption, The 19, 84–85, 92, 98, 102–104, 106, 110
Duncan, Walter 85

Ecumenical bodies 119–122
Ecumenical movement, The 21, 122–124
Erskine, Ebenezer 17–18, 53–56, 60, 66, 70, 74
Erskine, John 74–75
Erskine, Ralph 57–58, 60–61, 70–71, 74–75

First Book of Discipline, The 23, 27
Fisher, James 70–71, 74
Free Church Case 19, 106–108, 128
Free Presbyterians 109

Geddes, Jenny 36
George III 81
Gib, Adam 71, 74, 76–77, 81–82
Gillespie, Thomas 17–18, 61–62, 65–66
Glas of Tealing, John 80
Guthrie, James 40

INDEX

Hamilton, Patrick 24, 87
Henderson of Leuchers, Alexander 36, 49
Hunter, Josiah 77

indulgences 23-24, 42
Inverkeithing Case, The 64–65, 90

Jacobites 51, 90
James VI and I 16, 28, 30, 32–33, 37
James VII and II 44
Johnston of Warriston 36, 40, 49

Kirkmabreck Case, The 111–112
Knox, John 24-26

Lanark Case, The 62–63
Lifter Controversy, The 75–78
Lord High Commissioner 23, 102–103
Luther, Martin 23–24

Magna Carta of the Kirk 31
Marnoch Case, The 98–101
Marrow of Modern Divinity, The 60
Matthew, Patrick 74–75
Melville, Andrew 28–30, 32, 50
Melville, James 32
Moncrieff, Lord 14, 93–94
Morton, Earl of 28–29

New Licht Burghers, 78–79, 83
New Licht Controversy, The 78

Patronage, Abolition of 50–51
, Law of 17–19, 48, 50–52, 61, 89–90, 102
, Restoration of 51–53
Presbyterian Church of England, The 113
Presbytery of Relief 17, 65

Reformation 23–26, 29
Relief Church 66, 84
Renwick, James 44–45, 69
Reunion 83–85, 109
Revolution Settlement Act, The 13, 42, 45–46, 50–51, 58, 89, 94
Riding Committee, The 62–64, 90

Sanquar, Declaration of 43
Scots Confession of 1560, The 27, 50
Second Book of Discipline, The 29
Secession, The First 57–58, 86
       , Growth of the 69–70
       , The Second 65–67
Simson, John 59–60
Smyton, David 76–77
Solemn League and Covenant 39, 48–49, 60, 71
Stewarton Case 103
Stuart Kings 16, 40–43, 45, 51–52

Test Act, The 44
Toleration Act of 1711, The 51, 59
Torphichen Case, The 63–64, 90

United Free Church 10
United Free (Continuing) 109
United Presbyterian Church 17, 66, 84–85, 107
United Reformed Church 10
United Secession Church 83

Veto 19
Veto Act, The 92–95, 97, 99
Voluntaryism 81–82, 108

Wee Frees 107, 109
Westminster Assembly 48–50
Westminster Confession in the Church Today, The 49–50, 58–59, 78, 82, 108–109
Whitefield, George 70–72
William IV 51
William and Mary 45
Wishart, George 24
World Alliance of Reformed Churches 20, 120, 124
World Council of Churches, The 20, 119–122